THE OFFICIAL 2017/20

G000144819

WEST HAM UNITED

LONDON

HAMMERS
YEARBOOK

Written by twocan
Contributor: Peter Rogers
A TWOCAN PUBLICATION

©2017. Published by twocan under licence from West Ham United FC.

ISBN: 978-1-911502-34-0

3

CONTENTS

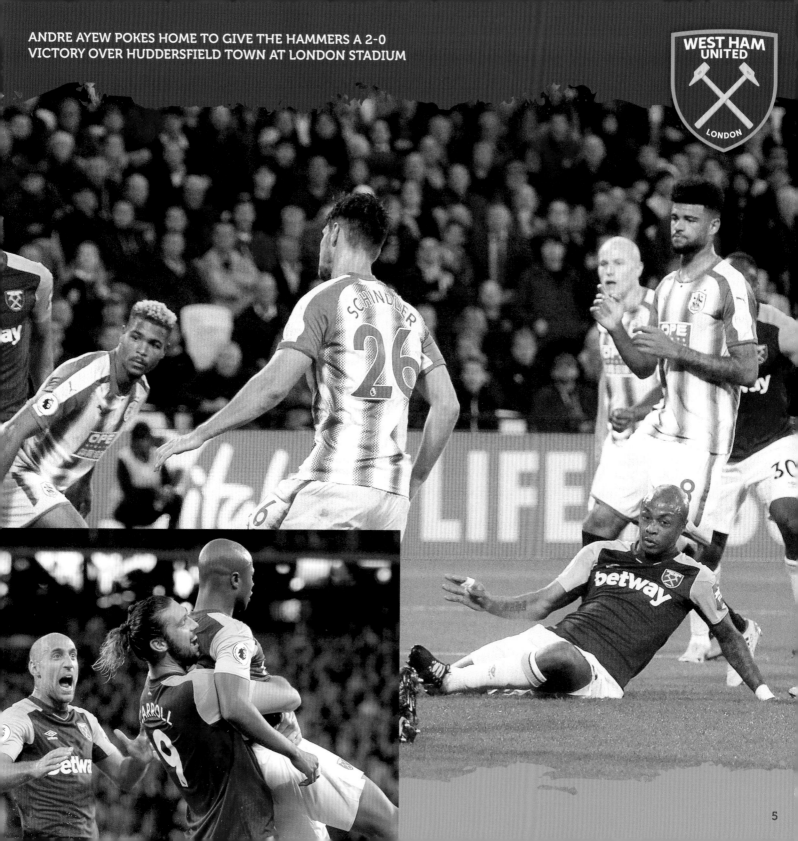

ANDRE AYEW POKES HOME TO GIVE THE HAMMERS A 2-0
VICTORY OVER HUDDERSFIELD TOWN AT LONDON STADIUM

2017/2018

AUGUST

Sunday	13	Manchester United	A	
Saturday	19	Southampton	H	
Wednesday	23	Cheltenham Town	A	Carabao Cup 2
Saturday	26	Newcastle United	A	

SEPTEMBER

Monday	11	Huddersfield Town	H	
Saturday	16	West Bromwich Albion	A	
Tuesday	19	Bolton Wanderers	H	Carabao Cup 3
Saturday	23	Tottenham Hotspur	H	
Saturday	30	Swansea City	H	

OCTOBER

Saturday	14	Burnley	A	
Friday	20	Brighton & HA	H	
Wednesday	25	Tottenham Hotspur	A	Carabao Cup 4
Saturday	28	Crystal Palace	A	

NOVEMBER

Saturday	04	Liverpool	H	
Sunday	19	Watford	A	
Friday	24	Leicester City	H	
Wednesday	29	Everton	A	

DECEMBER

Saturday	02	Manchester City	A	
Saturday	09	Chelsea	H	
Wednesday	13	Arsenal	H	
Saturday	16	Stoke City	A	
W/C	18			Carabao Cup 5
Saturday	23	Newcastle United	H	
Tuesday	26	Bournemouth	A	
Saturday	30	Tottenham Hotspur	A	

PREMIER LEAGUE FIXTURES

JANUARY

Monday	1	WBA	H	
Saturday	6			Emirates FA Cup 3
W/C	8	Semi-final first leg		Carabao Cup SF
Saturday	13	Huddersfield Town	A	
Saturday	20	Bournemouth	H	
W/C	22	Semi-final second leg		Carabao Cup SF
Saturday	27			Emirates FA Cup 4
Tuesday	30	Crystal Palace	H	

FEBRUARY

Saturday	03	Brighton & HA	A	
Saturday	10	Watford	H	
Saturday	17			Emirates FA Cup 5
Saturday	24	Liverpool	A	
Sunday	25			Carabao Cup Final

MARCH

Saturday	03	Swansea City	A	
Saturday	10	Burnley	H	
Saturday	17	Manchester United	H	Emirates FA Cup 6
Saturday	31	Southampton	H	

APRIL

Saturday	07	Chelsea	A	
Saturday	14	Stoke City	H	
Saturday	21	Arsenal	A	Emirates FA Cup SF
Saturday	28	Manchester City	H	

MAY

Saturday	05	Leicester City	A	
Sunday	13	Everton	H	
Saturday	19			Emirates FA Cup Final

FIXTURES ARE SUBJECT TO CHANGE

2017/2018 PREMIER LEAGUE

BACK ROW L-R: Domingos Quina, Sead Haksabanovic, Diafra Sakho, Antonio Martinez, Cheikhou Kouyate, Andy Carroll, Angelo Ogbonna, Marko Arnautovic, Edimilson Fernandes, Nathan Holland, Moses Makasi. CENTRE ROW: Julian Dicks, Chris Woods, Andre Ayew, Declan Rice, James Collins, Adrian, Joe Hart, Nathan Trott, Jose Fonte, Michail Antonio, Sam Byram, James Saban, Gary Lewin. FRONT ROW: Aaron Cresswell, Pedro Obiang, Pablo Zabaleta, Mark Noble, Edin Terzic, Slaven Bilic, Nikola Jurcevic, Miljenko Rak, Winston Reid, Javier Hernandez, Arthur Masuaku, Manuel Lanzini.

WEST HAM UNITED
LONDON

Winger Michail Antonio collected the prestigious Hammer of the Year award following the club's maiden season at the new London Stadium.

HAMMER OF THE YEAR

Having enjoyed two excellent seasons with the Hammers following his transfer from Nottingham Forest in September 2015, Antonio was certainly a fitting winner of the award at the end of this historic campaign - particularly after adding his name to the scoresheet in the final Premier League game at the Boleyn Ground and then scoring the first-ever Premier League goal at London Stadium.

On collecting the award, Antonio became the 39th different player to land the honour after winning the acclaim of the Claret and Blue Army.

The flying winger made an excellent start to the 2016/17 campaign - his goal in that first Premier League game at London Stadium sealed a 1-0 victory over Bournemouth and saw his name etched into the club's history books.

His early season displays saw him net five goals in four consecutive Premier League games. Such impressive form was rewarded with his first England call-up. After being included in the England squad for Sam Allardyce's only game in charge, he was included in the Three Lions squad for a second time, by Big Sam's successor Gareth Southgate in March.

The season ended with Antonio making 37 appearances in all competitions, scoring nine goals and registering five assists. He won 47 per cent of the Hammer of the Year vote, with Manuel Lanzini finishing as runner-up with 21 per cent, and Pedro Obiang third with 14 per cent.

"It's just a great feeling and hopefully I can do it again!" said the winger after collecting his award. "I'm extremely grateful to the fans who voted for me because they have been to home and away games, week-in, week-out, so for them to give this award to me has left me so overwhelmed.

"It's crazy because I've only been in the Premier League for two years and last year I came runner-up and this year I've won it, so hopefully I can keep going, keep pushing on and keep doing what I'm doing.

"I have to say my England call-up was a massive highlight and winning Hammer of the Year is amazing because it's come from the fans."

Antonio was clearly the star-turn at the Hammers' end of season awards event after landing the main prize. After being pipped to the top award by Antonio, Lanzini took home the Players' Player of the Year honour, Andy Carroll benefited from one of Antonio's aforementioned assists to net the Goal of the Season against Crystal Palace, while Darren Randolph's fingertip stop to deny Liverpool's Jordan Henderson scooped the Save of the Season award.

James Collins' display in the 1-0 win over Swansea City won the Best Individual Performance trophy, while the 2-1 EFL Cup victory over Chelsea at London Stadium was the Best Team Performance. Signing of the Season went to Edimilson Fernandes, while Young Hammer of the Year was Declan Rice and Domingos Quina won the Dylan Tombides Award.

MICHAIL**ANTONIO**

WEST HAM UNITED
LONDON

WEST HAM UNITE
HARLOW   LANGLE

CANNING TOWN E16

MANUEL LANZINI WEAVES HIS WAY THROUGH THE STURM GRAZ DEFENCE

PREPARATIONS

Ahead of their Premier League opener away to Manchester United, the Hammers played six pre-season fixtures in three countries as Slaven Bilic's men toured Austria, Germany and Iceland.

As always, the pre-season preparations were all geared around building up players' fitness levels, operating various different formations and experimenting with alternative patterns of play, while also integrating new players into the squad.

Once the squad had returned from their summer break, Bilic and his troops flew out to Austria for an eleven-day training camp which included two matches.

The first game of the pre-season schedule saw the Hammers record a goalless draw against Sturm Graz II at the Thermenstadion in Bad Waltersdorf, Austria on Monday 17 July.

The match saw summer signing Pablo Zabaleta in a West Ham shirt for the first time and game-time during this fixture was vital to the travelling squad. As a result eleven changes were made at the break giving every fit member of the squad a useful 45-minute work-out.

Despite creating several chances in both halves, Bilic's men couldn't find the breakthrough against young and spirited opponents.

More pleasing for the Hammers boss, however, was the fact that 22 of his players came through the encounter unscathed and all made a positive step forward in their fitness programmes during this important early period of pre-season training. After a number of gruelling sessions, on to game two of the pre-season programme. An all-English clash with Championship club Fulham on Thursday 20 July at the Sportzentrum in Graz-Weinzodl.

The match once again saw most members of the group gain valuable minutes as West Ham recorded a 2-1 win. Both Hammers goals came in a dominant first half. Manuel Lanzini opened the scoring on 14 minutes after manufacturing space for himself with a cute drop of the shoulder, then finding the bottom left-hand corner from 15 yards.

PABLO ZABALETA

2017/18 PRE-SEASON

Five minutes before the interval, Ashley Fletcher made it 2-0, robbing Fulham goalkeeper David Button as he tried to deal with a back-pass, leaving him the simple task of knocking the ball into an unguarded net.

The half-time interval once again saw Bilic rotate his squad, with only Josh Cullen playing more than 45 minutes. Fulham's Ryan Sessegnon pulled one back late on, but the Hammers held firm to ensure the Austrian leg of their European tour ended in victory.

Following the Austrian training camp, the Hammers continued their build-up to the new 2017/18 campaign in Germany with the Betway Cup meeting with Werder Bremen. The first leg was played on Friday, 28 July at Scheverdingen, Germany, with the second leg scheduled just 24 hours later.

Despite controlling possession for long periods and having virtual domination of the second half, the Hammers slipped to a 1-0 defeat. In front of 3,350 fans in Scheverdingen, 50 miles east of Werder's home city, the German side took a first-leg lead through teenage striker Johannes Eggestein's 12th-minute goal.

The match also saw record signing Marko Arnautovic make his first appearance in claret and blue against one of his former clubs. Bilic named a youthful starting line-up, with six players aged 21 or under and although the youngsters controlled possession for extended periods, they could not break down a well-marshalled defence.

Just a day after the first leg of the Betway Cup, the Hammers attempted to turn around the one-goal deficit when they played the second leg against Werder Bremen in the German town of Lohne.

On-loan Premier League striker Yuning Zhang scored the vital goal as Werder Bremen again edged West Ham to lift the Betway Cup. Zhang, who joined the Bundesliga club from West Bromwich Albion, struck the vital goal with just nine minutes remaining to secure Werder a 2-2 draw on the day and a 3-2 aggregate success.

Goals from debutant Marko Arnautovic and Toni Martinez had dragged West Ham back from two goals down after Luca Caldirola's powerful header had doubled Bremen's aggregate advantage on 15 minutes.

However, just when it looked like the Betway Cup might be decided by a penalty shootout, Swedish wing-back Ludwig Augustinsson cut the ball back and Zhang expertly steered his finish beyond the grasp of Joe Hart.

MARKO ARNAUTOVIC CELEBRATES SCORING AGAINST WERDER BREMEN

PREPARATIONS

So, two years after winning the Betway Cup with a 2-1 win at the Boleyn Ground, Werder repeated the feat with another narrow victory on home soil.

The Hammers' third and final game on German soil came when they faced Altona 93 in Hamburg on Tuesday 1 August, 2017. A crowd of around 5,000 were treated to a highly-entertaining 3-3 draw as the ten-man Hammers came from behind on three occasions to earn a spirited draw.

This final game in Germany saw a debut handed to recent signing Chicharito and a welcome return to action for Winston Reid after his injury lay-off, only for the latter to be shown a red card at the Adolf-Jager Kampfbahn.

However, goals from Toni Martinez and Andre Ayew and a Joshua Du Preez own-goal seconds after Chicharito's introduction, ensured West Ham shared the spoils with their German hosts.

The final leg of the European tour was completed as the team touched down in Iceland and history was made on Friday 4 August as the Hammers took on Manchester City in a first-ever fixture played between two Premier League clubs in Iceland.

An injury-depleted West Ham side gave their all against Pep Guardiola's men at Reykjavik's Laugardsvollur national stadium, but ultimately fell to goals from Brazilian Gabriel Jesus, Argentinian Sergio Aguero and England winger Raheem Sterling.

A near full-strength City deserved their win in front of a crowd 6,237. After an encouraging opening, West Ham were guilty of playing a part in their own downfall as Angelo Ogbonna and Arthur Masuaku got themselves in a muddle, allowing right-wing-back Danilo to steal possession. The summer signing from Real Madrid passed to Kevin De Bruyne, who crossed accurately for Jesus to convert from close range after just eight minutes.

From then on, City took the upper hand, keeping the ball for long periods, as has become their trademark under Guardiola. Further goals were added after the break from Aguero (53) and Sterling (71).

After a busy summer of recruitment, Bilic will have been more than satisfied with the way his latest signings had gelled into the group. The pre-season programme offered a number of challenges and opportunities, but most importantly, it provided the squad with an environment where they could prepare themselves physically, mentally and tactically for the long season ahead.

CHICHARITO

NATHAN HOLLAND V MAN CITY IN ICELAND

When it came to awarding the West Ham United Goal of the Season accolade for 2016/17 there really was only ever one show in town - Andy Carroll's breathtaking scissor-kick in the Hammers' 3-0 defeat of London rivals Crystal Palace at London Stadium in January 2017.

As most Hammers fans will have noted over the past five seasons, when Andy Carroll leads the attacking line the team has a unique presence and goal threat that others sides often cannot live with. That fact was perfectly demonstrated as Slaven Bilic's men swept the Eagles aside to record their first Premier League triumph of the calendar year.

The timing of both the victory and Carroll's audacious finish really could not have been better. The Hammers had started the New Year with back-to-back home defeats to both Manchester clubs, United in the Premier League and City in the FA Cup. Hence there was a real need and desire to return to winning ways on home soil.

After a hard fought opening half, the Hammers eventually engineered the breakthrough that their approach play to richly deserved as Sofiane Feghouli opened the scoring after 68 minutes. With the deadlock broken the visitors were forced to go in search of an equaliser and that in-turn left the Hammers with opportunities to attack on the counter.

It came as little surprise when the hosts doubled their lead eleven minutes from time, but the goal itself was simply one of those 'I was there' moments as Carroll dispatched his stunning finish.

The goal was created down the left-hand channel as Manuel Lanzini combined with Michail Antonio who floated a cross into the Palace box where Carroll peeled away from his marker before unleashing a stunning mid-air volley that left visiting 'keeper Wayne Hennessey helpless.

The footage remains there to be enjoyed time and time again on West Ham TV and the impressive facts behind the goal are that Carroll was 13.4 yards from goal when he struck the ball and he hit the shot was hit with a speed of 62.1 mph. Incredibly the ball was 5ft 10in off ground when struck and it took just 0.47 seconds to reach back of net.

With the stadium still buzzing from Carroll's wonder-strike, Lanzini wrapped up the win with the Hammers' third goal after 86 minutes.

The win was certainly welcome, but all the post-match talk surrounded Carroll's goal and the striker himself admitted it was his best ever.

ANDY CARROLL'S

GOAL
OF THE SEASON

*"It's been a while in the making - I've been trying for a couple of years.
It's got to be the best goal I've scored.*

WEST HAM UNITED LONDON

Winston **REID**

2

POSITION: Defender	**DATE OF BIRTH:** 03/07/1988
PLACE OF BIRTH: Auckland, New Zealand	

With over 200 appearances for the club, Winston Reid has become a vital member of the Hammers' squad and his presence in the team certainly brings a level confidence to those around him.

Reid made 36 appearances for Hammers last season and scored the only goal of the game to secure a vital 1-0 win over Sunderland at London Stadium in October 2016.

Initially recruited from Danish side FC Midtjylland in 2010, the big New Zealander has become a consistent performer with the ability to operate at right-back or as a central-defender.

His Hammers debut came against Aston Villa in August 2010 and he became a regular face in the side during the 2011/12 Championship campaign as the Hammers won promotion via the Play-Offs. The 2012/13 season was another memorable one for Reid as his outstanding performances at the heart of the defence saw him rewarded with the prestigious Hammer of the Year award. In March 2016, he agreed a new long-term contract at the club.

PREMIER LEAGUE SQUAD

3 Aaron **CRESSWELL**

POSITION: Defender	**DATE OF BIRTH:** 15/12/1989
PLACE OF BIRTH: Liverpool	

Despite a knee injury delaying his involvement in the club's 2016/17 campaign, once back to full fitness, Aaron Cresswell proved yet again to be a popular, committed and reliable member of the Hammers' squad.

He made 29 appearances in all competitions at club level where his outstanding form was rewarded with his international debut. Cresswell won his first England cap on 15 November 2016 when he replaced Danny Rose in the 2-2 draw with Spain at Wembley. He won a second cap in the end-of-season friendly away to France.

The Liverpool-born defender began his career at Tranmere Rovers where his impressive form saw him seal a move to Championship side Ipswich Town.

He joined the Hammers from Ipswich in July 2014 and soon made the left-back berth his own. A consistent performer with a desire to get forward, he was voted Hammer of the Year during his debut season with the club.

Jose **FONTE**

4

POSITION: Defender   **DATE OF BIRTH:** 22/12/1983

PLACE OF BIRTH: Penafiel, Portugal

Experienced Portuguese central-defender Jose Fonte joined the Hammers in the 2017 January transfer window following an £8M switch from Premier League rivals Southampton.

Despite suffering a 4-0 defeat against Manchester City on his debut, Fonte enjoyed a swift return to St Mary's in his second game for the club as the Hammers secured an excellent 3-1 away triumph. In total he played 16 games for the club last season following his mid-season transfer and helped the side achieve four Premier League clean-sheets.

After beginning his career in Portugal, he joined Crystal Palace on loan before securing a permanent move to Selhurst Park. He joined Southampton in 2010 and enjoyed two promotions as the Saints climbed from League One to the Premier League and also tasted Wembley glory in the Football League Trophy. In his seven years at Southampton, Fonte made 288 appearances and scored 15 goals.

A full Portugal international with over 25 caps to his name, Fonte was part of the Portugal squad that won the UEFA European Championships in 2016.

Pablo **ZABALETA**

5

POSITION: Defender   DATE OF BIRTH: 16/01/1985

PLACE OF BIRTH: Buenos Aires

Argentinean right-back Pablo Zabaleta joined West Ham United in May 2017 following nine trophy-laden seasons with Manchester City.

Very much the modern day full-back, Zabaleta combines his defensive duties with a real appetite to get forward and support the attack. With the Hammers operating with three central-defenders and wing-backs in the opening months of the new season, the 32-year-old has been able to slip seamlessly into a defensive unit with Aaron Cresswell taking the left-side wing-back berth and Zabaleta on his favoured right.

Born in Buenos Aires, Zabaleta began his career in his homeland with San Lorenzo before captaining the Argentinean U20 side to World Cup glory in 2005 and securing a big-money move to Espanyol in Spain. During his three seasons at Espanyol, Zabaleta was a Copa del Rey winner and UEFA Cup runner-up.

Despite reported interest from Juventus, he joined Manchester City in 2008 and went on to become a cult-hero at the Etihad Stadium. He made 333 appearances while residing in the blue half of Manchester and won two Premier League titles, one FA Cup, two League Cups and the Community Shield.

WEST HAM UNITED LONDON

Marko **ARNAUTOVIC** 7

POSITION: Forward	**DATE OF BIRTH:** 19/04/1989
PLACE OF BIRTH: Vienna, Austria	

West Ham completed the summer signing of Marko Arnautovic from Stoke City in a club record £20M-plus deal in July 2017.

Having starred at Premier League level with the Potters, where he scored 22 goals from 125 games and created numerous goals for teammates, his arrival at London Stadium has been seen as a real coup for the Hammers.

Arnautovic also boasts an impressive goals-to-games ratio at international level too with 15 goals for Austria from his 64 appearances as at the end of August 2017.

An extremely talented playmaker, who looks set to thrill the Hammers' fans at London Stadium and on their travels, Arnautovic began his professional career with FC Twente before spending the 2009/10 season on loan at Inter Milan. He joined German side Werder Bremen in June 2010 and it was his impressive performances in the Bundesliga that tempted Stoke to sign him for £2M in September 2013.

Cheikhou **KOUYATE**

8

POSITION: Midfielder	DATE OF BIRTH: 21/12/1989	
PLACE OF BIRTH: Daker, Senegal		

Senegalese international midfielder Cheikhou Kouyate wrote his name into the Hammers' history books by becoming the first player to score at the new London Stadium when he struck just eight minutes into the Hammers' 3-0 Europa League victory over Domzale.

One of the first names on the Hammers' team sheet in 2016/17, Kouyate made 36 appearances in all competitions and chipped in with a vital goal to secure a 1-0 win over Swansea City at London Stadium as the team ended a disappointing five-match losing run.

Signed from Anderlecht in June 2014, Kouyate has Europa League and Champions League experience to call upon and his powerful all-action displays have made him a popular figure with West Ham United fans.

He represented Senegal at the Africa Cup of Nations in January 2017 and will be hopeful of helping his country to qualify for the 2018 World Cup Finals in Russia.

WEST HAM UNITED LONDON

Andy **CARROLL**

9

POSITION: Forward	**DATE OF BIRTH:** 19/04/1989
PLACE OF BIRTH: Gateshead	

Andy Carroll gave the crowd at London Stadium a real moment to remember when he scored an outstanding mid-air volley in the 3-0 victory at home to Crystal Palace in January 2017.

The goal was certainly one of the highlights of the club's debut campaign at London Stadium and won Carroll both the national Goal of the Month award and the Hammers' Goal of the Season accolade.

After beginning his career with Newcastle United and securing a high profile transfer to Liverpool, Carroll joined West Ham in August 2012 on loan before agreeing a permanent switch in May 2013. Since joining the Hammers, Carroll has produced some outstanding displays and has become a firm fans favourite.

Injuries restricted Carroll to featuring in 18 Premier League fixtures last season where he netted seven goals. With such an impressive goals-to-games ratio the Hammers will be hopeful of seeing him lead the line on a regular basis in 2017/18.

PREMIER LEAGUE SQUAD

10 Manuel LANZINI

POSITION: Midfielder **DATE OF BIRTH:** 15/02/1993
PLACE OF BIRTH: Ituzaingo, Argentina

With 39 appearances in all competitions during the Hammers' 2016/17 campaign, no player featured in more games for the club last season than Argentinean midfielder Manuel Lanzini.

Hammers fans have been spoilt down the years with talented midfield playmakers such as Martin Peters, Sir Trevor Brooking and Alan Devonshire all donning the famous claret and blue shirt. Blessed with a wonderful eye for a pass, phenomenal dribbling ability and a real desire to run at opponents, Lanzini could well see his name added to the list of West Ham greats if his form continues in the same vein.

Lanzini proved a massive hit at the Boleyn Ground as his debut season in England ended with 31 appearances and a highly impressive seven goals. His form triggered the club into making his season-long loan a permanent transfer and his joined West Ham permanently in July 2016.

The 24-year-old picked up from where he left off as the new 2016/17 season got under way as he netted eight goals from his 39 appearances and was voted runner-up in the end-of-season Hammer of the Year award.

WEST HAM UNITED LONDON

2017/2018

ADRIAN

13

POSITION: Goalkeeper **DATE OF BIRTH:** 03/01/1987

PLACE OF BIRTH: Seville, Spain

Giant Spanish goalkeeper Adrian has made over 100 Premier League appearances for the Hammers since joining the club from Real Betis in July 2013.

A string of eye-catching performances saw him make the goalkeeper's shirt his own during the 2014/15 and 2015/16 campaigns. His form was rewarded with a new longer-term contract in October 2015.

The 2016/17 season began with a career highlight when he was included in Spain's squad for a friendly with Belgium and a World Cup 2018 qualifier with Liechtenstein. He also kept a clean-sheet in the Hammers' first Premier League win at London Stadium.

However, as the season progressed Adrian was forced to share goalkeeping duties with Darren Randolph. Adrian lost his place in the side following the 1-1 draw with Stoke City in November, but returned to the Premier League starting line-up at the tail end of the season and kept three back-to-back clean-sheets against Everton, Stoke City and Tottenham Hotspur.

PREMIER LEAGUE SQUAD

14

Pedro **OBIANG**

POSITION: Midfielder   **DATE OF BIRTH:** 27/03/1992

PLACE OF BIRTH: Alcala de Henares, Spain

Midfielder Pedro Obiang set the Hammers on their way to their first Premier League victory of the 2017/18 season when he opened the scoring against newly-promoted Huddersfield Town at London Stadium in September 2017.

The 2016/17 season saw Obiang cement his place in the Hammers' starting line-up and he netted his first goal for the club the highly impressive 3-1 victory over Southampton at St Mary's in February 2017.

An all-action former Spanish under-21 international, Obiang joined the Hammers from Sampdoria in the summer of 2015. He made 30 appearances for the club in all competitions during his debut season and late substitute appearances ensured that he featured in both the final game at the Boleyn Ground and the first game at London Stadium.

He featured in 30 first-team fixtures last season and looks all set to be a key player for the Hammers once again in 2017/18.

WEST HAM UNITED

15

Diafra **SAKHO**

POSITION: Forward   **DATE OF BIRTH:** 24/12/1989

PLACE OF BIRTH: Guediawaye, Senegal

A Senegalese teammate of Cheikhou Kouyate, forward Diafra Sakho joined the Hammers from French side FC Metz in August 2014.

After spending his entire professional career with Metz, he agreed a four-year deal with West Ham and enjoyed an impressive debut season for the club in 2014/15. A quick, strong and all-round quality athlete, Sakho was soon among the goals and ended the campaign as leading scorer with 12 goals from 26 appearances in all competitions.

Despite adding his name to the scoresheet in the historic final game at the Boleyn Ground in 2015/16, he was unable to replicate his goalscoring form of the previous season. Sakho was linked with a move away from the club in summer of 2016 and almost his entire 2016/17 season was sabotaged by a hamstring injury and then a back injury, which required surgery.

With his injury problems behind him, Sakho featured in the Hammers' opening five Premier League fixtures and was on target in the EFL Cup victories over Cheltenham Town and Bolton Wanderers as he looks to make up for lost time in 2017/18.

PREMIER LEAGUE SQUAD

16

Mark **NOBLE**

POSITION: Midfielder   **DATE OF BIRTH:** 08/05/1987

PLACE OF BIRTH: Canning Town

Popular Hammers captain Mark Noble made 35 appearances and scored five goals in 2016/17 as the club adjusted to life at London Stadium.

During a five-match spell without a Premier League victory leading into December 2016, Noble stepped up to the plate and scored the only goal of the game in back-to-back home victories over Burnley and Hull City. So often the Hammers' saviour, Noble netted on the stroke of half-time to help defeat Burnley on December 14 and then calmly dispatched a second-half penalty with his usual level of efficiency to see off the Tigers three days later.

An inspirational character around the club, skipper Noble is the club's longest-serving player among the current squad, having made his Hammers debut back in 2004 and was voted Hammer of the Year in both 2011/12 and 2013/14.

Noble's loyalty to the club was rewarded with a memorable testimonial fixture at the Boleyn Ground in March 2016 when the Hammers took on a side of West Ham United all-stars on a memorable afternoon in front of a crowd of over 35,000.

Javier **HERNANDEZ** **17**

POSITION: Forward	**DATE OF BIRTH:** 01/06/1988
PLACE OF BIRTH: Guadalajara, Mexico	

Known more commonly by his nickname of 'Chicharito' - the Hammers landed the goalscoring skills of Javier Hernandez from Bayer Leverkusen in July 2017 for a fee of £16M.

With two Premier League titles to his name following a successful spell with Manchester United, Hernandez brings a proven goalscoring track record to London Stadium. His arrival also underlines the club's desire to recruit players with Premier League experience, with his signing coming on the back of the successful recruitment of Joe Hart, Pablo Zabaleta and Marko Arnautovic.

Hernandez, who is Mexico's all-time record goalscorer, wasted little time in showing the Hammers' faithful what he is capable of as he scored twice in only his second game for the club as West Ham suffered a narrow 3-2 defeat at Southampton.

Undoubtedly viewed as the 20-goal-a-season front-man that the Hammers crave, Hernandez will be looking for impressive club form in 2017/18, before heading off to Russia where he will lead the line for Mexico in the World Cup Finals.

PREMIER LEAGUE SQUAD

James COLLINS

19

POSITION: Defender   DATE OF BIRTH: 23/08/1983

PLACE OF BIRTH: Newport

After being part of the Wales squad that took Euro 2016 by storm, central-defender James Collins certainly started the 2016/17 Premier League in fine form and netted the Hammers' first league goal of the season.

His 77th-minute goal against champions Chelsea at Stamford Bride looked to have secured a valuable point for West Ham until a last minute Diego Costa winner broke Hammers hearts.

With the ability to operate as one of two central defenders or as part of a back three with wing-backs, Collins continues to feature with consistent reliability for both club and country.

Now in his second spell with West Ham, Collins began his career with Cardiff City before joining the Hammers for the first time in 2005. In his first spell at the Boleyn Ground he helped the club reach the FA Cup final in 2006 and battle successfully against relegation in 2007. After three years with Aston Villa, Collins joined the club for a second time in August 2012.

Andre **AYEW**

20

POSITION: Forward	**DATE OF BIRTH:** 17/12/1989	
PLACE OF BIRTH: Seclin, France		

The arrival of Ghanaian international forward Andre Ayew from Swansea City for a then club record fee of £20.6M in the summer of 2016 certainly sparked a great deal of excitement among the Hammers faithful.

Ayew made his debut in the opening game of the 2016/17 Premier League campaign away to Chelsea, but after just half-an-hour of action he suffered a serious groin injury which sidelined him for over two months.

His return to action was ironically against the Blues when the two sides were paired with one another in the EFL Cup fourth round - this time the Hammers came out on top with a 2-1 victory. Ayew netted his first goal for the club in the 4-1 Boxing Day rout away to his former employers, but his progress in a Hammers shirt was then cut short by his involvement in Ghana's Africa Cup of Nations campaign.

He enjoyed a promising end to the season with five Premier League goals in the Hammers' final 13 fixtures including netting the club's final goal of the 2016/17 season away to Burnley.

Angelo **OGBONNA** 21

POSITION: Defender   **DATE OF BIRTH:** 23/05/1988

PLACE OF BIRTH: Cassino, Italy

Powerful Italian defender Angelo Ogbonna was greatly missed in the final third of the 2016/17 season, as knee surgery ruled him out of action for all of February, March and April before he returned to the side on the final day of the season as the Hammers won 2-1 at Burnley.

A strong and mobile central-defender who also has the flexibility to operate at left-back, Ogbonna won back-to-back Italian titles with Juventus prior to joining the Hammers in July 2015.

He enjoyed a winning debut as the Hammers triumphed 2-0 at Arsenal on the opening day of the 2015/16 season and made 34 appearances in his first season at the club. Ogbonna was very much the hero of the hour in the FA Cup Fourth Round Replay against Liverpool at the Boleyn Ground, as he picked the perfect time to head home his first goal in claret and blue to seal a memorable 2-1 extra-time victory.

A regular in the side at the start of the 2017/18 campaign, he scored his first goal of the season the 3-0 EFL Cup triumph over Bolton Wanderers at London Stadium in September.

WEST HAM UNITED LONDON

Sam **BYRAM**

22

POSITION: Defender **DATE OF BIRTH:** 16/09/1993
PLACE OF BIRTH: Thurrock

A hamstring injury ruled young defender Sam Byram out of action between October 2016 and January 2017 which certainly interrupted his first full season with the Hammers.

Bryam started all four Europa League ties and therefore featured in the club's opening game at London Stadium as the Hammers defeated NK Domzale 3-0. He was also involved in five of the team's opening seven Premier League fixtures before the unfortunate timing of his injury.

He returned to full fitness and made his comeback appearance in the 3-0 home victory over Crystal Palace. The former Leeds United man then enjoyed an extended run in the side, starting ten of the club's final 17 Premier League games.

A pacey right-back and swift in the tackle, Byram featured in both of the Hammers' 2017/18 EFL Cup triumphs as West Ham eliminated Cheltenham Town and Bolton Wanderers and kept clean-sheet on both occasions.

WEST HAM UNITED LONDON

23 Sead HAKSABANOVIC

POSITION: Midfielder   **DATE OF BIRTH:** 04/05/1999
PLACE OF BIRTH: Hyltebruk, Sweden

West Ham's 3-0 EFL Cup victory over Bolton Wanderers at London Stadium in September 2017 witnessed talented midfielder Sead Haksabanovic make his first-team debut for the club.

The Montenegro attacking midfielder became West Ham United's fifth signing of the summer transfer window when he arrived in east London on 7 August 2017.

The exciting 18-year-old joined the Hammers on a five-year contract for an undisclosed fee from Swedish club Halmstads BK, where he became the second-youngest player in Allsvenskan league history in April 2015. Prior to his first-team debut against Bolton, Haksabanovic had also featured in the under-21 side's Football League Trophy victory away to Swindon Town.

Blessed with searing pace, outstanding technical ability and an eye for goal, Swedish-born Haksabanovic had already made 70 first-team appearances and made his senior international debut in May 2017 prior to moving to England.

25

Joe **Hart**

POSITION: Goalkeeper   DATE OF BIRTH: 19/04/1987

PLACE OF BIRTH: Shrewsbury

The Hammers pulled off a major transfer coup in the summer of 2017 when they secured the services of England goalkeeper Joe Hart on a season-long loan from Manchester City.

A highly rated 'keeper with a plethora of honours from his time at the Etihad Stadium, Hart adds an exceptional level of experience to the Hammers' squad. He began his career with local side Shrewsbury Town where his talents soon alerted a host of top clubs, including Manchester City who secured his services in 2006. Hart gained useful experience with loan stints at Tranmere Rovers, Blackpool and Birmingham City before establishing himself as City's number one.

A popular figure with the Manchester City fans, Hart won two Premier League titles, two League Cups and the FA Cup with the Citizens before spending last season on loan at Torino.

With the World Cup finals in the summer on the horizon, Hart will be aiming to excel at Premier League level with the Hammers and then head out to Russia as Gareth Southgate's first choice stopper.

PREMIER LEAGUE SQUAD

WEST HAM UNITED LONDON

26

Arthur **Masuaku**

POSITION: Defender   **DATE OF BIRTH:** 07/11/1993
PLACE OF BIRTH: Lille, France

Two frustrating knee injuries prevented French defender Arthur Masuaku from really showing the West Ham faithful his true potential during a challenging first season at the club.

After enjoying two title-winning seasons in Greece with Olympiacos, the highly-rated young defender joined the Hammers in August 2016 for a fee of £6.2M. He made his Premier League debut in the opening fixture of the season away to Chelsea and also started West Ham's first Premier League game at the new London Stadium as the Hammers overcame Bournemouth 1-0.

Masuaku then suffered a knee injury in the EFL Cup tie with Accrington Stanley in September 2016 which ruled him out of contention until November. He returned to the team in December, but a further knee problem sidelined him until late February 2017.

In total he made 15 first team appearances in 2016/17, but has already made a positive start to the new season and scored his first goal for the club in the 3-0 victory over Bolton Wanderers in the EFL Cup.

PREMIER LEAGUE

30

Michael **Antonio**

POSITION: Midfielder **DATE OF BIRTH:** 28/03/1990

PLACE OF BIRTH: Wandsworth

Flying winger Michail Antonio enjoyed a memorable 2016/17 campaign that ended with him collecting the coveted Hammer of the Year award.

West Ham United competed the signing of Antonio from Championship side Nottingham Forest in September 2015. The London-born winger enjoyed a highly-successful debut season with the Hammers in 2015/16 that ended with nine goals - eight of which came in the Premier League.

He started life at the new London Stadium with the same scintillating form that he showed when saying farewell to the Boleyn Ground and netted the club's first Premier League goal at the new stadium as the team secured a memorable 1-0 victory over Bournemouth. His impressive early-season form in 2016/17 resulted in an England call-up but he has yet to make his international debut.

Antonio ended last season with 37 appearances, nine goals and five assists. He was duly presented with the Hammer of the Year award and signed a new long-term contract in May 2017.

Edimilson
FERNANDES

31

POSITION: Midfielder	**DATE OF BIRTH:** 15/04/1996
PLACE OF BIRTH: Sion, Switzerland	

Young midfielder Edimilson Fernandes enjoyed an eventful first season at London Stadium in 2016/17 having joined West Ham United in August 2016 from Swiss Super League side FC Sion.

After agreeing a four-year deal with the Hammers, Fernandes made his first-team debut in the EFL Cup victory over Accrington Stanley, before going on to taste Premier League action with a late substitute appearances at home to Southampton. His first Premier League start coincided with a vital 1-0 win over Sunderland at London Stadium in October 2016.

Fernandes won the hearts of the West Ham fans when he scored what proved to be the winning goal in the EFL Cup fourth round tie at home to London-rivals Chelsea.

In his three years as a professional at Sion, Fernandes won his international recognition with Switzerland at under-21 level. Since joining West Ham and playing in the Premier League he has been called up to the senior Switzerland squad and made his debut for them against the Faroe Islands in November 2016.

Declan **Rice**

25

POSITION: Midfielder	**DATE OF BIRTH:** 14/01/1999
PLACE OF BIRTH: London	

Promising midfielder Decaln Rice made his Hammers' debut in the closing stages of the final game of the 2016/17 season as West Ham ran out 2-1 winners away to Burnley.

With the ability to operate as either a holding midfielder or central defender, Rice joined the Hammers' Academy at under-14 level, having previously been with Chelsea.

The young Irishman is highly rated among the coaching staff at the Academy and has enjoyed a host of excellent performances while progressing through the ranks at youth team and development squad level.

His first-team exposure has continued to gather pace in the early stage of the 2017/18 campaign as he featured in all four of the club's opening Premier League fixtures including starts away to Southampton and Newcastle United. He also played 90 minutes in both of West Ham's successful EFL Cup ties against Cheltenham Town and Bolton Wanderers.

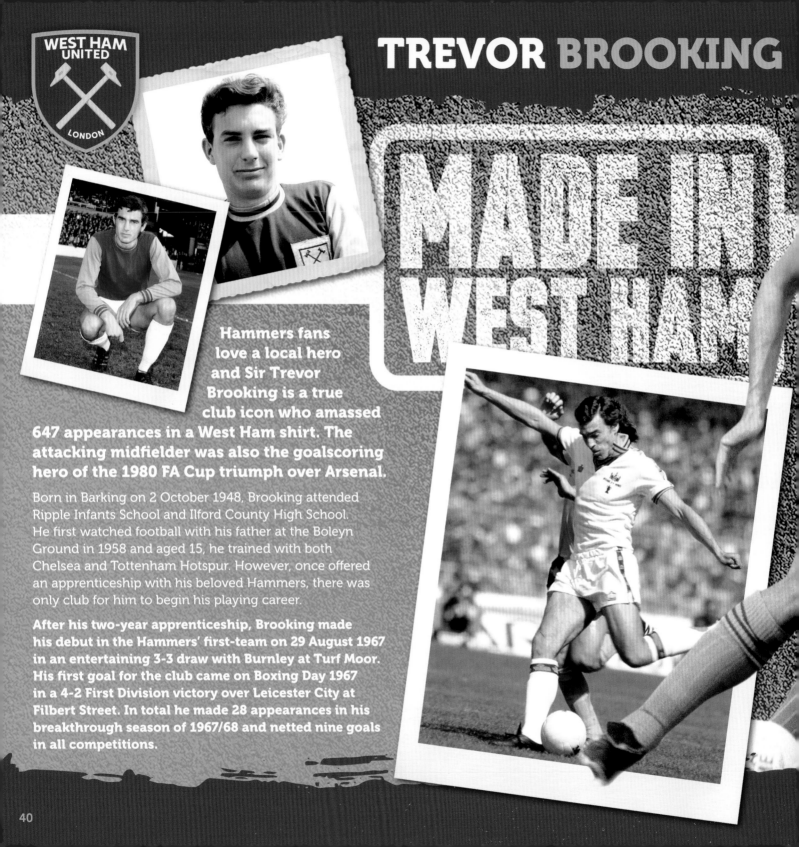

TREVOR BROOKING

MADE IN WEST HAM

Hammers fans love a local hero and Sir Trevor Brooking is a true club icon who amassed 647 appearances in a West Ham shirt. The attacking midfielder was also the goalscoring hero of the 1980 FA Cup triumph over Arsenal.

Born in Barking on 2 October 1948, Brooking attended Ripple Infants School and Ilford County High School. He first watched football with his father at the Boleyn Ground in 1958 and aged 15, he trained with both Chelsea and Tottenham Hotspur. However, once offered an apprenticeship with his beloved Hammers, there was only club for him to begin his playing career.

After his two-year apprenticeship, Brooking made his debut in the Hammers' first-team on 29 August 1967 in an entertaining 3-3 draw with Burnley at Turf Moor. His first goal for the club came on Boxing Day 1967 in a 4-2 First Division victory over Leicester City at Filbert Street. In total he made 28 appearances in his breakthrough season of 1967/68 and netted nine goals in all competitions.

With a wonderful eye for a pass, Brooking became a controlling influence on the team in what would become one of the greatest eras in the club's history. Brooking learned a great deal from playing alongside Martin Peters and was awarded the first of his five Hammer of the Year awards in 1971/72.

He was twice an FA Cup winner, firstly in 1975, when the Hammers defeated fellow Londoners Fulham in the final and again in 1980 when he headed home the only goal of the game to defeat the favourites, Arsenal.

Brooking also played in two Charity Shield matches for the club, the 1976 European Cup-Winners' Cup Final and was also a vital member of the club's 1980/81 Second Division title-winning team.

After 647 appearances and 102 goals for the club, his playing career ended on 18 May 1984 in a 1-0 home defeat to Everton. Only Billy Bonds, Bobby Moore and Frank Lampard (Senior) have played more games for West Ham United.

After a distinguished career for both club and country, Brooking became a well respected TV pundit and a figure of authority when it came to the future development of the game. He joined the Hammers board and has twice stepped up to briefly become caretaker manager.

West Ham through and through, Brooking is very much viewed as the Barking-boy made good.

WEST HAM UNITED
LONDON

16/17 REVIEW

CHEIKHOU KOUYATE CELEBRATES HIS SECOND OF THE NIGHT AGAINST NK DOMZALE

ANDY CARROLL'S FIRST V JUVENTUS

WELCOME TO WEST HAM UNITED

'00 West Ham United FC

1964 FA Cup Winners · 1965 European Cup Winners' Cup · 1975 FA Cup Winners · 1980 FA Cup Winners

THE MAGNIFICENT LONDON STADIUM HOSTS THE HAMMERS' FIRST COMPETITIVE MATCH AGAINST SLOVENIA'S NK DOMZALE IN THE EUROPA LEAGUE

The Hammers' 2016/17 season began with a Europa League qualifier in Slovenia and ended with a 2-1 Premier League victory at Burnley - suffice to say there were plenty of twists and turns along the way as the club played its first season at London Stadium.

Slaven Bilic's men began their competitive fixtures with a Europa League third qualifying round tie against NK Domzale in late July and were left with work to do in the second leg after falling to a 2-1 defeat in Slovenia. However, the narrow defeat certainly set things up perfectly for the club's eagerly awaited opening game at London Stadium.

In front of a crowd of 54,000 a Cheikhou Kouyate double and a maiden strike for Sofiane Feghouli crowned a historic night for West Ham United at their new home as a 3-0 win secured progression to the play-off stages of the Europa League.

The club officially opened the new Stadium with a prestigious fixture against Italian giants Juventus in the Betway Cup in August, a week before the start of the Premier League Season. The occasion was marked by an opening ceremony before the kick-off, which was a fitting tribute to the Hammers' new home.

Despite beginning the 2016/17 Premier League campaign with an agonising late 2-1 defeat away to champions Chelsea, West Ham marked their opening league game at the London Stadium with a victory. Michail Antonio stole the headlines as he scored a dramatic late winner to hand West Ham their first Premier League victory at their new home with a 1-0 win over Bournemouth.

MICHAIL ANTONIO'S WINNER AGAINST AFC BOURNEMOUTH

August ended with a 2-1 aggregate defeat to Astra Giurgiu and elimination from the Europa League plus a 3-1 defeat to early-season pacesetters Manchester City in the Premier League.

16/17 REVIEW

betway

WINSTON REID SECURED THREE POINTS AGAINST THE BLACK CATS

A DELIGHTED MANUEL LANZINI AFTER HIS WINNER AT SELHURST PARK

CHEIKHOU KOUYATE WITH THE FIRST AGAINST LONDON RIVALS CHELSEA IN THE EFL CUP

September certainly proved to be a challenging month for the club with three straight Premier League defeats leaving the Hammers at the wrong end of the table. Watford followed in Astra Giurgiu's footsteps by winning at London Stadium, before a second 4-2 defeat in a week arrived at West Bromwich Albion. Progression in the EFL Cup was won after a 1-0 victory over Accrington Stanley before the month closed with a 3-0 defeat at home to Southampton.

Fortunately, October proved to be a far better month as the Hammers got back into the winning habit.

A 1-1 draw at home to newly-promoted Middlesbrough was achieved following a memorable solo-effort from Dimitri Payet. Then after the international break, Bilic's side secured their first away win of the season.

The Hammers welcomed back Aaron Cresswell for his first appearance of the season away to Crystal Palace. A gritty defensive performance at Selhurst Park saw the team capitalise on Manuel Lanzini's first-half strike to take all three points, despite the late dismissal of Cresswell.

A last-gasp Winston Reid goal proved enough to secure back-to-back Premier League wins as Sunderland were defeated 1-0 at London Stadium. Next up was an EFL Cup tie at home to Chelsea and on a memorable evening, the Hammers edged past their London rivals 2-1 to land a place in the fifth round draw. Although the month ended with a 2-0 defeat at Everton, the cup triumph and improved league results gave the club a major boost.

The fixture computer had presented the Hammers with a tough schedule in November and the EFL Cup draw had not been too kind either with Bilic's men forced to return to Old Trafford for a cup tie just three days after their Premier League fixture on the same ground. The month began with a hard-fought 1-1 draw at home to Stoke City, before two late Harry Kane goals sentenced the Hammers to a 3-2 defeat on their final visit to White Hart Lane.

Off to Manchester for the league and cup double-header with United and Diafra Sakho gave the travelling fans an early boost as his second minute goal put the Hammers in front at Old Trafford. Despite Zlatan Ibrahimovic's equaliser, the Hammers produced a resolute display to win a useful point. Avoiding defeat at Old Trafford twice in the space of four days proved to be a bridge too far as the EFL Cup campaign ended with 4-1 defeat.

As is so often the case, the hectic December schedule can be a vital period of the season and so it proved for the Hammers who won three consecutive Premier League games over the festive period.

16/17 REVIEW

A heavy home defeat to Arsenal was followed by an excellent performance away to Liverpool as goals from Payet and Antonio helped secure a 2-2 draw. Once again Mark Noble then proved to be the Hammers' man-of-the-moment as he scored the only goal of the game in the next two home fixtures to secure crucial 1-0 wins over Burnley and Hull City.

Hammers fans were then treated to the perfect Christmas present as a devastating display of finishing secured a 4-1 win at Swansea before the calendar year of 2016 ended with a narrow 1-0 defeat at 2015/16 champions Leicester City.

The New Year began with a record crowd at London Stadium for the 2-0 defeat at the hands of Manchester United. Any hopes of an FA Cup run were swiftly ended as Manchester City ran out 5-0 winners following their third round visit to London Stadium. This topsy-turvy campaign was then followed by two excellent Andy Carroll-inspired wins - he stuck the Hammers' goal of the season in a 3-0 victory at home to Crystal Palace before netting a brace in the 3-1 away win at Middlesbrough. The month was dominated by the ongoing antics of want-away star Payet who finally sealed a £25M move back to Marseille at the end of January as the Hammers secured the signing of Hull City midfielder Robert Snodgrass.

February got off to the best possible start with Carroll once again on target in a fine 3-1 win away to Southampton before creditable draws at home to West Brom and away to Watford completed the Hammers' February programme.

A disappointing run of five defeats throughout March and into April finally came to an end when Kouyate netted the only goal of the game to seal a much needed victory over Swansea City at London Stadium. April ended with the team proving difficult to beat again as honours ended even with Sunderland, Everton and Stoke.

The final month of the season witnessed a fantastic 1-0 London derby victory at home to Spurs. The home campaign ended with a defeat to Liverpool before the season concluded with a 2-1 at Burnley.

MANUEL LANZINI CELEBRATES THE WINNER AT HOME TO SPURS

An eleventh-place finish was achieved following the win at Turf Moor and on reflection the 2016/17 season was one of mixed fortunes for West Ham United.

WEST HAM UNITED LONDON

MICHAIL ANTONIO HITS THE BACK OF THE NET AT ANFIELD

ANDRE AYEW WITH THE WINNER AT BURNLEY

The highlights being the outstanding home win over Spurs and the battling performances at Old Trafford and Anfield

47

PREMIER LEAGUE KEY PLAYERS

With some of the very best talent in world football currently plying their trade in the Premier League, we've selected one player from each of the other 19 Premier League squads to keep tabs on over the coming months.

AARON RAMSEY · ARSENAL

A star performer in Wales' Euro 2016 heroics, Arsenal midfielder Aaron Ramsey is widely regarded as one of the best attacking midfielders in the Premier League. A real box-to-box player who has so often been the Gunners' match winner. He scored Arsenal's winning goal in last season's FA Cup final triumph over Chelsea and got the new 2017/18 season off to a bang with a goal in the thrilling 4-3 opening night victory over Leicester City.

ASMIR BEGOVIC · BOURNEMOUTH

Bosnia and Herzegovina international 'keeper Asmir Begovic joined Bournemouth in the summer of 2017 from Premier League Champions Chelsea and is expected to make the No.1 shirt his own at the Vitality Stadium. His arrival on the south coast was seen as a real coup for Cherries' boss Eddie Howe. Begovic gained an excellent reputation as a quality Premier League performer with Stoke City before his move to Stamford Bridge and Cherries fans will be looking for him to repeat the superb form he showed with the Potters at his latest club.

ANTHONY KNOCKAERT BRIGHTON & HA

Anthony Knockaert enjoyed a memorable 2016/17 season when his match-winning performances helped propel Brighton to the Premier League. Knockaert was the Sky Bet Championship player of the season as the Seagulls won promotion and returned to the top flight for the first time since 1982/83. An attacking wide man with a real eye for goal, Knockaert chipped in with 15 goals for Chris Hughton's side last season and is sure to be relishing the opportunity of showing what he can do at Premier League level in 2017/18.

A series of memorable performances for the Republic of Ireland in France at Euro 2016 helped seal Robbie Brady's move back to the Premier League in January 2017. A real dead-ball specialist, midfielder Brady joined the Clarets from Norwich City in a reported £13M deal. His arrival at Turf Moor saw him link-up with international teammates Jeff Hendrick and Stephen Ward. After joining the Clarets, Brady soon demonstrated just why boss Sean Dyche was so keen to secure his services - marking his home debut with a memorable free-kick to secure a point against Chelsea.

ROBBIE BRADY · BURNLEY

THIBAUT COURTOIS
CHELSEA

Goalkeeper Thibaut Courtois was certainly a key performer for Chelsea in last season's Premier League title-winning campaign. He will once again be one of the first names on the Chelsea teamsheet as the Blues attempt to retain their crown in 2018. His giant frame and razor sharp instincts, coupled with excellent distribution skills, breed confidence in the players around him. The big Belgian is also sure to be his country's first choice goalkeeper in the World Cup finals in Russia.

TOMMY SMITH
HUDDERSFIELD TOWN

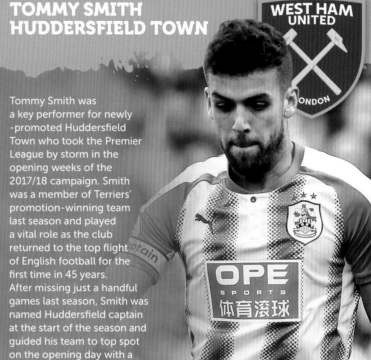

Tommy Smith was a key performer for newly-promoted Huddersfield Town who took the Premier League by storm in the opening weeks of the 2017/18 campaign. Smith was a member of Terriers' promotion-winning team last season and played a vital role as the club returned to the top flight of English football for the first time in 45 years. After missing just a handful games last season, Smith was named Huddersfield captain at the start of the season and guided his team to top spot on the opening day with a 3-0 victory at Crystal Palace.

CHRISTIAN BENTEKE
CRYSTAL PALACE

Powerful Belgian striker Christian Benteke plundered an impressive 15 Premier League goals in his debut season at Selhurst Park as Palace secured Premier League status. Despite a challenging start to the 2017/18 season for the Eagles, Benteke continues to link up well with Wilfried Zaha and if the two of them hit top form they are sure to cause a host of problems for Premier League defenders. Benteke will be keen to impress new boss Roy Hodgson and enjoy a positive season at club level before performing in the World Cup finals.

JORDAN PICKFORD
EVERTON

All eyes will be on Jordan Pickford following his big-money move from Sunderland in the summer. The highly-rated stopper enhanced his growing reputation with a number of outstanding displays for Sunderland despite the Black Cats' relegation in 2016/17. After an exciting summer of new arrivals at Goodison Park, great things are expected of Pickford and a new-look Everton side in what should be an exciting season for the Toffees both at home and in Europe.

JAMIE VARDY · LEICESTER CITY

Star striker Jamie Vardy scored the goals that fired the Foxes to their memorable Premier League title-winning triumph in 2015/16 and the Leicester City front-man has become one of the Premier League's most revered strikers. He began the new 2017/18 season in sparkling form with five Premier League goals from his first six matches. Vardy will be looking for a goal-filled 2017/18 campaign as he prepares to cement his place in the England squad for the World Cup finals in Russia.

JORDAN HENDERSON
LIVERPOOL

All-action midfielder Henderson joined Liverpool form Sunderland in June 2011 and became the Reds' captain in 2015 following the departure of Steven Gerrard. Widely recognised as the real heartbeat of the Liverpool midfield engine room, Jordan has now played over 200 games for the Anfield club. His energetic performances have made him a popular figure on Merseyside and the 27-year-old appears all set to be a key player for both club and country with the World Cup finals beckoning in the summer.

ROMELU LAKAKU
MANCHESTER UNITED

If Red Devils' striker Romelu Lakaku can continue his early-season goalscoring form, following his summer transfer from Everton, then the big Belgian is likely to have a serious say in just where the Premier League title ends up come May. United splashed out a massive transfer fee to land Lakaku in the summer and with a flying start to his Old Trafford career, it certainly looks to be money wisely spent by Jose Mourinho. A star turn at international level, Lakaku already has over 20 goals for Belgium to his name.

JACOB MURPHY
NEWCASTLE UNITED

A flying winger who can operate down either channel, Jacob Murphy joined Premier League new-boys Newcastle United in July 2017 from Norwich City, for a fee believed to have been in the region of £12M. Murphy enjoyed a breakthrough season at Carrow Road last term, scoring nine goals and winning international recognition with England U21s. Winning a regular first-team place for the Magpies will be a tough challenge, but if given the opportunity, Murphy certainly appears to have the skills to thrill at St. James' Park.

KYLE WALKER
MANCHESTER CITY

England international right-back Kyle Walker made a £45M move from Tottenham Hotspur to Manchester City in July 2017. An attacked-minded full-back, Walker loves to get forward to supply balls into dangerous areas for goalscoring teammates. His pace and power is sure to be a real asset for Pep Guardiola's title-chasing team. Walker is another player who will certainly be looking for a positive season at club level before boarding the England plane to Russia for the 2018 World Cup Finals.

Fraser Forster played in every one of Southampton's Premier League fixtures in 2016/17 and the England international is sure to be another important figure for the Saints again in this term. His huge physical presence fills the goal and makes him an imposing figure for opposition strikers and the reliable 'keeper agreed a new five-year deal at St Mary's in July 2017. Along with Jack Butland, Jordan Pickford and Tom Heaton, Forster will compete with the Hammers' on-loan 'keeper Joe Hart for the England goalkeeper's shirt at the 2018 World Cup finals.

FRASER FORSTER · SOUTHAMPTON

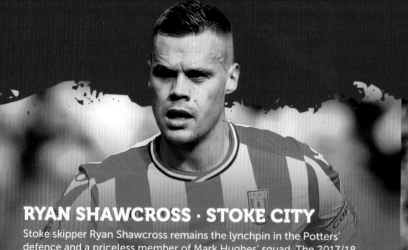

RYAN SHAWCROSS · STOKE CITY

Stoke skipper Ryan Shawcross remains the lynchpin in the Potters' defence and a priceless member of Mark Hughes' squad. The 2017/18 campaign will mark his testimonial season at the club. A fearless defender whose popularity with the club's fans grows and grows, he has now played over 350 times for Stoke City. The defender missed just three matches of the Potters' 2016/17 campaign as the club secured a respectable 13th placed finish in the Premier League.

KYLE NAUGHTON SWANSEA CITY

A much-travelled defender, Kyle joined Swansea City in January 2015 from Spurs. The speedy right-back is swift in the tackle and with good distribution skills, Naughton is very much the modern day full-back who loves to surge forward into attacking areas. He has the ability to operate as a traditional full-back or in the wing-back role should the Swans look to play with three central-defenders. The 28-year-old played a key role in the Swans' dramatic Premier League survival last season.

HARRY KANE · SPURS

Spurs and England striker Harry Kane has ended the last two seasons as the Premier League's leading scorer and has helped Spurs qualify for the Champions League on both occasions. A Tottenham fan, turned club captain, Kane is idolised by the White Hart Lane faithful and will be a serious contender to win the golden boot for a third consecutive season come May 2018. He began the 2017/18 season in sparkling form and looks set to be England's first choice striker at the 2018 World Cup finals.

ANDRE GRAY WATFORD

Striker Andre Gray completed a summer switch from Burnley to Watford for a Hornets' club record fee believed to have been around £18M. Gray has enjoyed a dramatic rise through the football pyramid having been a prolific scorer for Luton Town, Brentford and Burnley. He notched an impressive nine Premier League goals for the Clarets last season including a memorable hat-trick in a 4-1 demolition of Sunderland. New Watford boss Marco Silva will be looking for Gray to pick up at Vicarage Road just where he left off at Turf Moor.

GARETH McAULEY WEST BROMWICH ALBION

Reliable centre-half Gareth McAuley appears to simply get better and better with age. After a memorable Euro 2016 campaign, the Northern Ireland international was a standout performer for Tony Pulis' Baggies side in 2016/17 and even chipped in with six Premier League goals. Providing form and fitness remain, he's sure to be one of Pulis' go-to men once again during the 2017/18 season. McAuley will turn 39 in December 2018 and his vast experience at both domestic and international level continues to be of great benefit to both the Baggies and Northern Ireland.

2016/2017 SEASON QUIZ

WEST HAM UNITED — LONDON

The 2016/2017 season heralded an exciting new era for West Ham United FC

What can you recall of the Hammers' first campaign at London Stadium?

1 Who took the mantel of scoring the West Ham's first competitive goal at London Stadium?

2 Which player scored the club's first Premier League goal of 2016/17?

3 Against which team did the Hammers record their first Premier League win in 2016/17?

4 Can you name the League Two club that West Ham were paired with in the third round of the EFL Cup?

5 How many home Premier League fixtures did the team win during their London Stadium debut season?

6 Can you recall the two West Ham goalscorers from the 2-1 EFL Cup victory over London rivals Chelsea?

7 Against which club did striker Andy Carroll score his first goal of the season?

8 Which visiting side were the first opposition to record an away victory at London Stadium?

9 Can you name the three clubs that the Hammers recorded a Premier League double over in 2016/17?

10 The highest attendance at London Stadium in 2016-17 was 56,996 - can you name the opposition?

11 Forward Michail Antonio was the club's top scorer in 2016/17. How many goals did he net in all competitions?

12 Who made the most Premier League appearances between the sticks, Adrian or Darren Randolph?

13 Which midfielder progressed through the Academy to make his first-team debut on the final day of the 2016/17 season?

14 Which Championship club did Reece Oxford join on loan in the second-half of the season?

15 In which fixture did Diafra Sakho score his only goal of the campaign?

16 Can you name the Spanish club that loaned striker Simone Zaza left the Hammers for in January 2017?

17 Against which country did Aaron Cresswell make his England debut in November 2016?

18 During the January transfer window, the Hammers signed Scottish international Robert Snodgrass from which club?

19 Who was the Hammers' top Premier League appearance maker in 2016/17?

20 Who was crowned Hammer of the Year at the end of the first season at London Stadium?

WEST HAM UNITED
LONDON

ANSWERS ON PAGE 82

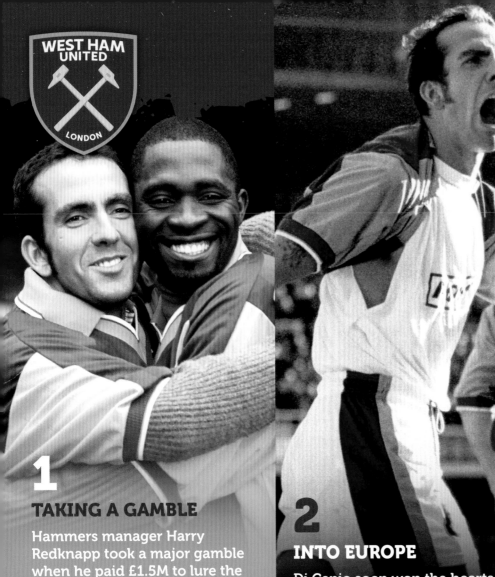

PAOLO DI CANIO'S SIX STEPS TO STARDOM

CONFIRMING HIS STATUS AS A TRUE HAMMERS LEGEND

1

TAKING A GAMBLE

Hammers manager Harry Redknapp took a major gamble when he paid £1.5M to lure the controversial Italian forward Paolo Di Canio to West Ham.

He arrived at the Boleyn Ground in January 1999 following a lengthy ban for pushing over referee Paul Alcock while at Sheffield Wednesday.

It certainly proved a gamble worth taking as Di Canio became one of the most popular Hammers stars of the modern era.

2

INTO EUROPE

Di Canio soon won the hearts and minds of the Hammers faithful and scored his first goal for the club in his fourth outing during a 2-0 victory over Blackburn Rovers.

He made 13 Premier League appearances following his arrival in the middle of the 1998/99 season and his five goals and countless assists helped the Hammers to a fifth place Premier League finish, that in-turn saw the club qualify for the UEFA Cup through the Intertoto Cup.

3

GOAL OF THE SEASON

Di Canio provided the fans with many memorable moments. Hammers boss Harry Redknapp once said; "He can do things with the ball that other people can only dream of."

One of those special moments came in March 2000 when he netted an outstanding flying volley against Wimbledon at the Boleyn Ground.

The goal won the BBC Goal of the Season award and is widely regarded as one of the most spectacular goals in Premier League history.

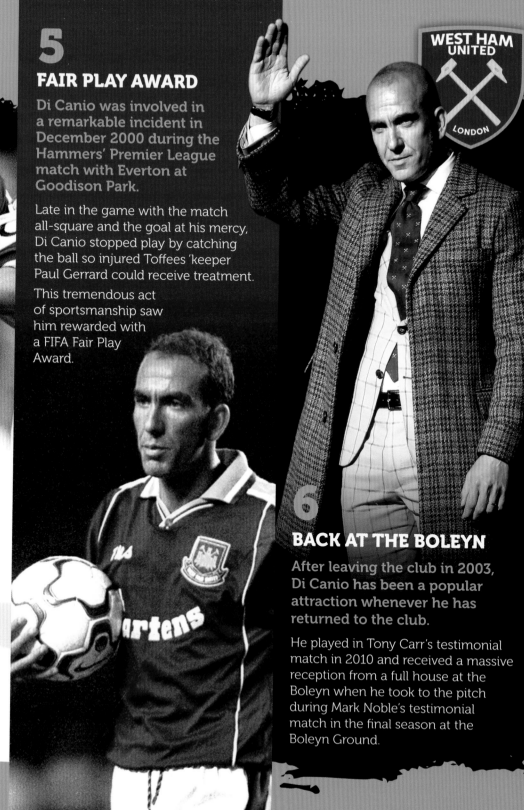

5
FAIR PLAY AWARD

Di Canio was involved in a remarkable incident in December 2000 during the Hammers' Premier League match with Everton at Goodison Park.

Late in the game with the match all-square and the goal at his mercy, Di Canio stopped play by catching the ball so injured Toffees 'keeper Paul Gerrard could receive treatment.

This tremendous act of sportsmanship saw him rewarded with a FIFA Fair Play Award.

4
HAMMER OF THE YEAR

With 18 goals, including the aforementioned Goal of the Season against Wimbledon, Di Canio was the club's top scorer and played a massive role in the club's ninth -place finish in the Premier League.

His 16 Premier League goals remain a record haul for any West Ham player in the Premier League and Di Canio was subsequently rewarded with the Hammer of the Year award at the end of the 1999/2000 campaign.

6
BACK AT THE BOLEYN

After leaving the club in 2003, Di Canio has been a popular attraction whenever he has returned to the club.

He played in Tony Carr's testimonial match in 2010 and received a massive reception from a full house at the Boleyn when he took to the pitch during Mark Noble's testimonial match in the final season at the Boleyn Ground.

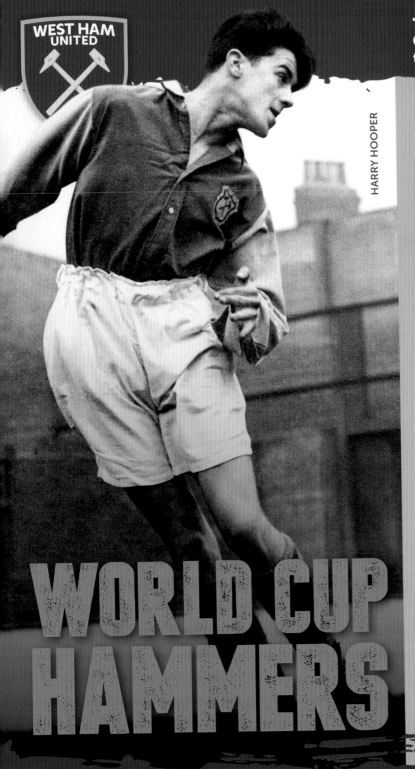

WEST HAM UNITED

HARRY HOOPER

WORLD CUP HAMMERS

The famous West Ham United trio of Bobby Moore, Geoff Hurst and Martin Peters propelled England to World Cup glory back in 1966...

...and next summer a number of current Hammers stars will go in search international success with their respective counties in Russia 2018.

Under the outstanding leadership of Bobby Moore, England savoured their finest hour on 30 July 1966 as a Geoff Hurst hat-trick and a Martin Peters goal led to skipper Moore holding aloft the Jules Rimet trophy on an unforgettable afternoon at Wembley following the 4-2 triumph over West Germany.

Those three West Ham United and England legends will always remain synonymous with English football's finest hour and the club is rightly proud of its major contribution to the country's success in '66. Although none have enjoyed the level of success and glory of Moore, Hurst and Peters, there are several other Hammers who have proudly represented their countries at the World Cup finals.

Aged just 21, Bobby Moore was the first West Ham player to feature in the World Cup finals when he was named in Walter Winterbottom's squad for the 1962 finals in Chile. However, that honour was almost taken by Hammers forward Harry Hooper who was named in the 22-man squad for Switzerland in 1954. Back then only 17 of the 22 travelled, with Hooper one of the five players placed on reserve status and remained at home awaiting a call if the need arose.

Moore played alongside Maurice Norman in Chile as England progressed from Group Four after losing to Hungary, defeating Argentina and drawing with Bulgaria. However, their interest in the tournament ended in the knockout stages when they were defeated 3-1 by the tournament's eventual winners, Brazil.

Four years later saw Moore, Hurst and Peters strut their stuff on home soil as England won their one and to-date only international tournament.

BOBBY MOORE, MAURICE NORMAN AND RON FLOWERS AFTER
DEFEATING ARGENTINA 3-1 IN CHILE 1962

GEOFF HURST HITS ENGLAND'S THIRD

ENGLAND AND WEST HAM CAPTAIN BOBBY MOORE
HOLDS ALOFT THE JULES RIMET WORLD CUP TROPHY

WORLD CUP

BOBBY MOORE 1970

TREVOR BOOKING
V SPAIN 1982

ALVIN MARTIN
V PARAGUAY 1986

FRANK MCAVENNIE CAUSING
PROBLEMS FOR THE WEST GERMAN DEFENCE

Come the 1970 finals in Mexico, with Peters now a Tottenham player, Moore and Hurst were left to fly the West Ham flag as England went in defence of their crown. This time West Germany gained revenge for their Wembley final defeat with a 3-2 victory over England at the quarter-final stage.

Following the 1970 finals in Mexico, the Hammers were not represented in the World Cup finals until Trevor Brooking featured in Ron Greenwood's England squad for Spain in 1982. Injury limited him to a substitute appearance in the second group stage as England drew 0-0 with the host country. That result eliminated England from the competition and proved to be Brooking's final international appearance.

Central defender Alvin Martin missed out on a trip to Spain with club teammate Brooking due to injury, but four years later, he got to taste World Cup finals action in Mexico 1986. Martin played in the 3-0 victory over Paraguay in the knockout stage as two goals from Gary Lineker and one from Peter Beardsley set-up the famous 'Hand of God' quarter-final meeting with Argentina.

Striker Frank McAvennie was another Hammer who played at Mexico '86 with the Glaswegian making two appearances in the finals. He came off the bench as Scotland lost to Denmark and West Germany. McAvennie's two outings at the finals made him the first non-English West Ham United player to feature at the World Cup finals.

After Martin and McAvennie's outings in Mexico '86, no Hammers appeared in the World Cup finals for 16 years until Joe Cole, Trevor Sinclair and David James were all named in England's 2002 squad for the finals in South Korea and Japan. Both Cole and Sinclair featured in the Three Lions' campaign while James was understudy to David Seaman.

HAMMERS

Under the guidance of manager Sven Goran Eriksson, it was a successful tournament for England who bowed out at the quarter-final stage after a 2-1 defeat to the eventual winners Brazil in Shizuoka on 21 June.

Hammers goalkeeper Shaka Hislop was the club's single representative at the 2006 finals in Germany. After playing for West Ham in the thrilling 2006 FA Cup final against Liverpool, his season concluded with two appearances in the finals for Trinidad and Tobago who drew 0-0 with Sweden and lost 2-0 to England in their Group B fixtures.

With more and more overseas players choosing to ply their trade in the English Premier League, the Hammers together with most top-flight English clubs, have seen a real cosmopolitan feel develop among their playing staff. As a result five Hammers players from four different countries were packing their bags for the 2010 finals in South Africa.

Goalkeeper Rob Green and defender Matt Upson both represented England, the latter on target with England's consolation goal as they were thrashed 4-1 by Germany in the knockout stage. Forward Guillermo Franco featured in all of four of Mexico's games while Switzerland's Valon Behrami had only a brief taste of the action in South Africa after being sent-off in his country's 1-0 defeat to Chile. Jonathan Spector was included in the USA squad but did not feature in any of their four fixtures.

The most recent Hammer to feature in the World Cup finals was Colombian midfielder Pablo Armero who played in four of his country's fixtures in the 2014 finals in Brazil as Colombia reached the quarter-finals. He was also on the score-sheet in Colombia's opening Group C match as they defeated Greece 3-0.

The scene is now set for the club's current crop of international players to step forward and etch their name into the history books for representing their country at a World Cup finals while playing their club football for West Ham United.

ROB GREEN

SHAKA HISLOP CELEBRATES AFTER TRINIDAD & TOBAGO'S DRAW WITH GERMANY IN 2006

GUILLERMO FRANCO

COLOMBIA'S PABLO ARMERO

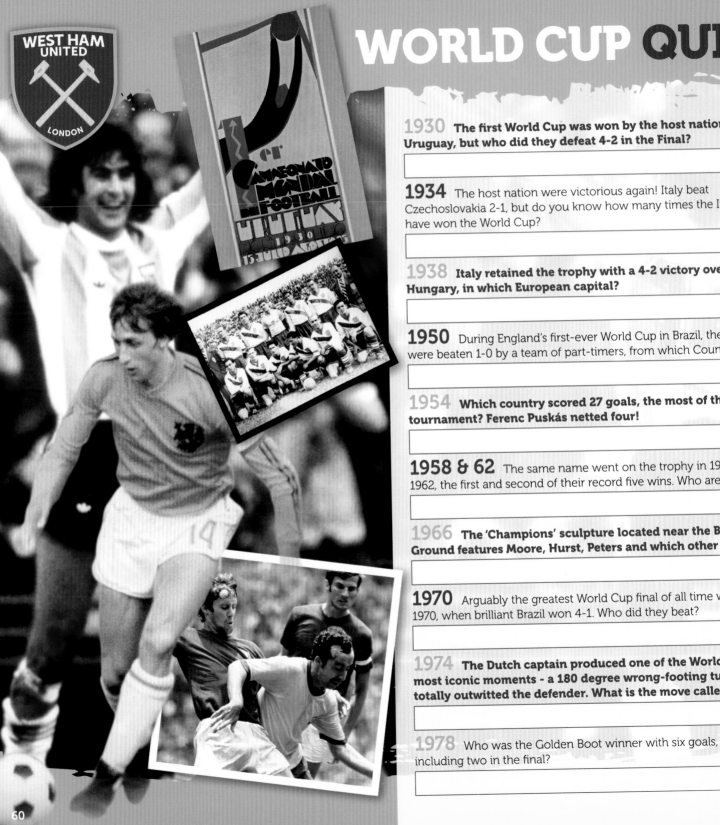

WORLD CUP QUIZ

1930 The first World Cup was won by the host nation Uruguay, but who did they defeat 4-2 in the Final?

1934 The host nation were victorious again! Italy beat Czechoslovakia 2-1, but do you know how many times the Italians have won the World Cup?

1938 Italy retained the trophy with a 4-2 victory over Hungary, in which European capital?

1950 During England's first-ever World Cup in Brazil, they were beaten 1-0 by a team of part-timers, from which Country?

1954 Which country scored 27 goals, the most of the tournament? Ferenc Puskás netted four!

1958 & 62 The same name went on the trophy in 1958 and 1962, the first and second of their record five wins. Who are they?

1966 The 'Champions' sculpture located near the Boleyn Ground features Moore, Hurst, Peters and which other player?

1970 Arguably the greatest World Cup final of all time was in 1970, when brilliant Brazil won 4-1. Who did they beat?

1974 The Dutch captain produced one of the World Cup's most iconic moments - a 180 degree wrong-footing turn that totally outwitted the defender. What is the move called?

1978 Who was the Golden Boot winner with six goals, including two in the final?

1982 Which Hammers legend played his last game for England in the 0-0 draw with Spain which resulted in England's elimination from the tournament?

1986 Which legendary Argentinian scored twice to knock England out at the quarter-final stage 2-1?

1990 In the opening match, the holders Argentina suffered a shock 1-0 defeat by which African nation?

1994 The record for most goals in a single match by one player is five, scored by Oleg Salenko as Cameroon were crushed 6-1 by which nation?

1998 Who won the Golden Ball award for the tournament's best player?

2002 This German star scored a hat-trick in the 8-0 demolition of Saudi Arabia - the first of his record 16 goals in World Cup finals. Who is he?

2006 One match, nicknamed 'the Battle of Nuremberg' ended nine-a-side as 16 yellow cards and four red cards were handed out. Who were the teams and what was the result?

2010 Which West Ham star was England's joint top-scorer in South Africa?

2014 Which country staged the last World Cup in 2014 and who are the World Cup holders?

2018 Where are the World Cup finals going to be held next summer?

ANSWERS ON PAGE 82

WEST HAM UNITED
LONDON

PREMIER LEAGUE 2

TUNJI AKINOLA

POSITION: Defender   **DOB: 21.11.98**

Centre-back Tunji Akinola has been with the Hammers since he was eight years old. The defender is now a regular for the U23 side.

MARCUS BROWNE

POSITION: Midfielder   **DOB: 18.12.97**

Browne is an exciting attacker, and made his first-team debut in August 2016, coming on as a substitute in the Europa League against Astra Giurgiu.

REECE BURKE

POSITION: Defender   **DOB: 02.09.96**

Currently on loan in the Championship with Bolton Wanderers, boyhood Hammers fan Burke made his senior debut for the Club in the FA Cup in 2014.

JOSH CULLEN

POSITION: Midfielder   **DOB: 07.04.96**

Ireland U21 international Cullen, who is on loan with Bolton Wanderers, is an all-action midfielder and was Bradford City's Players' Player of the Year on loan there in 2016/17.

GRADY DIANGANA

POSITION: Midfielder   **DOB: 19.03.98**

Tricky winger Diangana, who has been at the West Ham since he was ten, has been a regular in the U23 squad for the last two-and-a-half seasons.

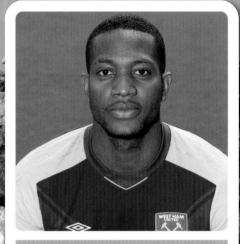

DONEIL HENRY

POSITION: Defender   **DOB: 20.04.93**

Full Canada international defender Henry signed the Club in 2015 after a spell in Cyprus. The centre-back spent part of 2016/17 on loan in Denmark.

JAHMAL HECTOR-INGRAM

POSITION: Forward   **DOB: 11.11.98**

Centre-forward Hector-Ingram is an out-an-out goalscorer. His record for the U18s in 2015/16 and 2016/17 has led to a number of starts for the U23s.

NATHAN HOLLAND

POSITION: Midfielder   **DOB: 19.06.98**

Holland left home-town club Everton in January 2017 for the Hammers. The exciting winger made his West Ham debut against Bolton in the Carabao Cup in September.

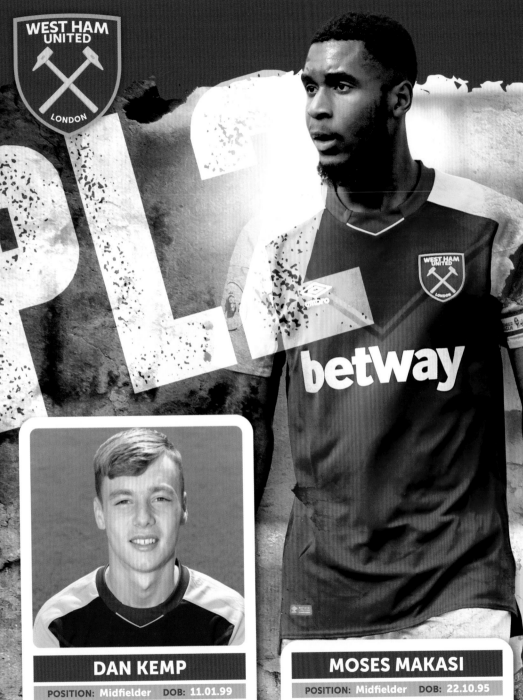

DAN KEMP

POSITION: Midfielder   **DOB:** 11.01.99

Kemp left Chelsea for West Ham in November 2015 and has excelled in east London. The winger is now an England U19 international and Toulon Tournament winner.

MOSES MAKASI

POSITION: Midfielder   **DOB:** 22.10.95

The U23s' captain, Makasi is the longest-serving player in the Club's Academy of Football. The midfielder was on the bench for the senior team twice in 2016/17.

TONI MARTINEZ

POSITION: Forward   **DOB:** 30.06.97

Forward Martinez moved to London in the summer of 2016, joining from Spanish giants Valencia. The striker was the U23 squad's top scorer in the 2016/17 campaign.

RIHARDS MATREVICS

POSITION: Goalkeeper   **DOB:** 18.03.99

Giant goalkeeper Matrevics is the U23s' current back-up stopper. The 6ft 7in teenager is also a Latvia U19 international.

VASHON NEUFVILLE

POSITION: Defender   **DOB:** 18.07.99

Full-back Neufville is an exciting prospect who represented England at U16 and U17 level. The left-sider first broke into the U23 side back in 2015.

JOSH PASK

POSITION: Defender   **DOB:** 01.11.97

Experienced Academy defender Pask joined West Ham in June 2006. The centre-back enjoyed a successful loan spell at Gillingham in League One in 2016/17.

ALEX PIKE

POSITION: Defender   **DOB:** 08.02.97

Versatile defender Pike has established himself as a key player for the U23s during the last few seasons. The natural right-back went on loan to Cheltenham Town in 2017.

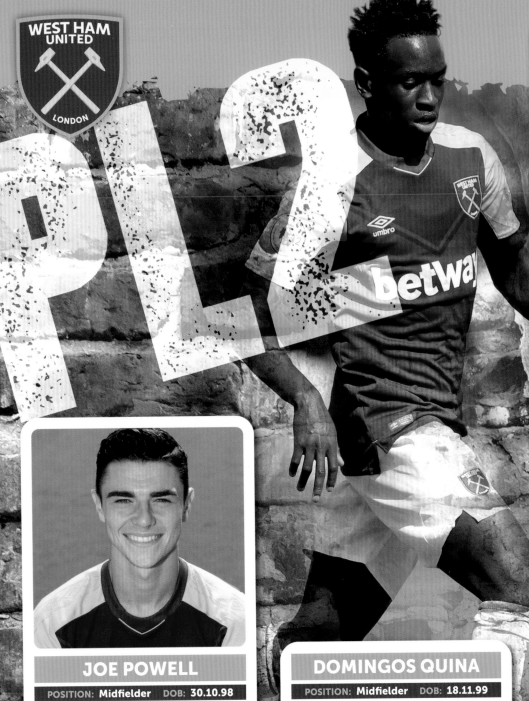

JOE POWELL

POSITION: Midfielder   **DOB:** 30.10.98

Winger Powell joined the Hammers when he was just eight-years-old. After a great run of form for the U18s, he began to feature for the U23s in during the second half of last season.

DOMINGOS QUINA

POSITION: Midfielder   **DOB:** 18.11.99

Quina joined the Hammers prior to the 2016/17 season. The exciting midfielder made his first team debut in the Europa League in 2016 and is a Portugal U20 international.

MARTIN SAMUELSEN

POSITION: Midfielder   **DOB:** 17.04.97

Full Norway international Samuelsen traded Manchester City for the Hammers in 2015. The tricky winger scored his first senior goal for his country against San Marino in October 2016.

ANTHONY SCULLY

POSITION: Midfielder   **DOB:** 03.12.99

Scully is a highly-rated midfielder who first signed for the Hammers in May 2011. He has earned international recognition, representing the Republic of Ireland up to U20 level.

NOHA SYLVESTRE

POSITION: Midfielder   **DOB:** 29.12.97

Midfielder Sylvestre is the son of former Switzerland international Patrick, who played at the 1994 World Cup. Noha is a versatile midfielder, who can also play at the back.

NATHAN TROTT

POSITION: Goalkeeper   **DOB:** 21.11.98

Trott is now the Club's third-choice goalkeeper, and is the U23s' No1. The stopper is a gifted England U20 international who is as good with the ball at his feet as in his hands.

The longest-serving player among the current West Ham squad, midfielder and captain Mark Noble is a real one-club warrior who remains an inspirational figure among the Hammers faithful.

Born in Canning Town, East London on 8 May 1987, Noble played youth football for Barking Colts and also trained at the Arsenal Academy when he was eleven.

He later joined the Hammers' Academy and swiftly progressed through the ranks. Such was his progress that he became the youngest player to appear in the club's reserve team, making his debut at that level aged only 15.

An all-action midfielder, his first-team debut arrived in a League Cup tie at home to Southend United in August 2004 as a Marlon Harewood brace sealed a 2-0 victory. After appearing in the 2004/05 Play-Off final victory over Preston North End at Wembley, replacing Shaun Newton as an 82nd-minute substitute, Noble found Premier League opportunities hard to come by in 2005/06 and took in brief loan spells with Hull City and Ipswich Town in a bid to gain additional first-team experience.

The 2007/08 season saw Noble really establish himself in the Hammers' first-team and he has never looked back. Voted Hammer of the Year in 2012 and 2014, Noble was back at Wembley for a second successful Play-Off final in 2012 as the club returned to the Premier League at the first time of asking following victory over Blackpool.

MADE IN WEST HAM

WEST HAM UNITED LONDON

Fittingly, Noble's testimonial season coincided with the final season at the Boleyn Ground in 2015/16.

For his testimonial on Monday 28 March 2016, an amazing 35,036 Hammers fans turned up to salute their long-serving captain's commitment to the club. The fixture saw a West Ham XI take on a team of Hammers all-stars in what was not only a celebration of Noble's career, but also a wonderful opportunity to see a host of club legends return to the Boleyn Ground during the famous old ground's farewell season.

All those who attended were treated to a trip down memory lane as faces new and old took to the field. Noble, celebrating twelve years in West Ham's first-team and flanked by his young children Honey and Lenny, took to the hallowed turf through a guard of honour made up of his current and former teammates, standing either side in West Ham's home and away colours.

The fact that so many former West Ham United greats returned to participate in the match, clearly demonstrated that the affection Noble receives from the club's supporters is equally matched by the respect for him among his playing peers.

As at the end of the 2016/17 season, Noble had made 402 appearances for the club and scored 48 goals. A modern day local-hero at the Boleyn Ground and London Stadium, he is sure to add to those impressive statistics in 2017/18 and beyond.

FAN'TASTIC

ANSWERS ON PAGE 82.

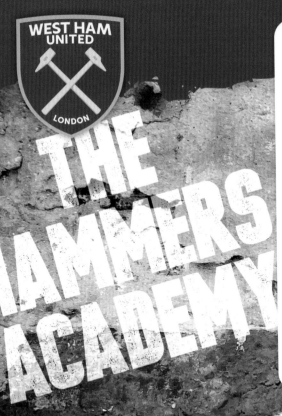

THE HAMMERS ACADEMY

AJIBOLA ALESE

POSITION: Defender   **DOB:** 17.01.01

Centre-back Alese made his U23 debut against Everton in the opening league game of 2017/18. He joined West Ham United as an eight-year-old.

KRISTIJAN BELIC

POSITION: Midfielder   **DOB:** 25.03.01

Serbian Belic is a talented defensive midfielder, who can pass as well as he can tackle. He was recently called-up to play for Serbia's U17 side.

SEAN ADARKWA

POSITION: Forward   **DOB:** 11.10.00

Powerful forward Adarkwa has been with the Club since November 2011. He impressed on a number of mid-season trips abroad during the 2016/17 campaign.

MASON BARRETT

POSITION: Defender   **DOB:** 24.09.99

Defender Barrett was another to join the Hammers when he was just eight. Versatile, the teenager can play anywhere across the back four.

YIANNIS CONSTANTINOU

POSITION: Forward   **DOB:** 14.12.99

Constantinou is a Greek attacker who can play either in midfield or up top in attack. He broke into the U18s in 2016/17 and remains a squad player this campaign.

CONOR COVENTRY

POSITION: Midfielder   **DOB:** 23.03.00

Republic of Ireland youth international Coventry recently signed his first professional contract with the Club in 2017. The midfielder plays for his country's U17s.

ANOUAR EL MHASSANI

POSITION: Midfielder   **DOB:** 18.04.01

Exciting attacking talent El Mhassani left Ajax in the summer of 2017 and relocated to join West Ham. The left-footed midfielder spent eight years with the Amsterdam outfit.

REECE HANNAM

POSITION: Defender   **DOB:** 11.09.00

Youngster Hannam was recently called up to an England youth camp. He made his competitive debut for the U23s in a vital end-of-season clash at West Brom in 2017.

KEVIN DALIPI

POSITION: Defender   **DOB:** 22.01.01

Kevin Dalipi has been at the Club only four years, but is a regular in the U18 matchday squads. The teenager's natural position is centre-back.

MALYK HAMILTON

POSITION: Midfielder   **DOB:** 02.09.99

Pacey winger Hamilton is a left-sider who joined the Hammers in October 2011. He represented Canada's U18s in 2016, making his debut against El Salvador.

KORREY HENRY

POSITION: Forward   **DOB:** 28.11.99

One of the U18s' key players, Henry is a powerful player who can play anywhere across the midfield or attack. He signed for West Ham back in April 2011.

THE HAMMERS ACADEMY

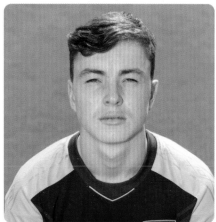

ALFIE LEWIS

POSITION: Midfielder **DOB:** 28.09.99

Lewis penned his first professional contract in the summer of 2017. A dictator at the heart of the midfield, the teenager has made a number of appearances for the U23s.

ROSAIRE LONGELO

POSITION: Midfielder **DOB:** 20.10.99

Left-sider Longelo can play on either flank and has also been utilised as a left-back. The pacey youngster is a regular starter for the U18 side.

BEN JOHNSON

POSITION: Midfielder **DOB:** 24.01.00

Midfielder Johnson is an attacking winger, but was utilised as a full-back by the U23s at the start of the 2017/18 campaign. A home appearance against Liverpool was his U23 debut.

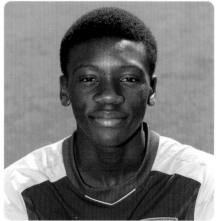

EMMANUEL LONGELO

POSITION: Midfielder **DOB:** 27.12.00

Brother of fellow Academy player Rosaire, midfielder Longelo joined in March 2011. He recently made his U23 debut, playing the last few minutes of an away clash in Sunderland.

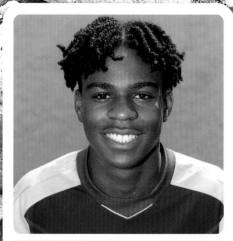

JAY MINGI

POSITION: Midfielder **DOB:** 22.10.00

Defensive midfielder Mingi put pen to paper at West Ham United when he was just eight-years-old. Mingi broke into the U18 squad in the 2016/17 season.

JEREMY NGAKIA

POSITION: Midfielder   **DOB:** 07.09.00

Ngakia is one of the newest players at the Academy, having joined only three years ago. The youngster is primarily a midfielder but can also operate at right-back.

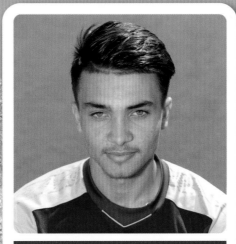

ODYSSEAS SPYRIDIS

POSITION: Midfielder   **DOB:** 17.01.01

Spyridis is a Cypriot attacker who can play either as a forward-thinking midfielder or a centre-forward. He has become a regular in the U18 matchday squads this campaign.

BERNARDO ROSA

POSITION: Midfielder   **DOB:** 20.09.00

Brazilian Rosa is a midfielder with plenty of flair. He signed his two-year scholarship with the Club in May 2017 and is a regular for the U18 side.

LOUIE WATSON

POSITION: Midfielder   **DOB:** 06.07.01

Watson is a midfielder who has been with the Club since August 2012. The teenager likes to get forward and was recently called up to an England youth training camp.

BEN WELLS

POSITION: Defender   **DOB:** 29.02.00

Boyhood Hammers fan Wells has been a Season Ticket Holder at the Club since he was a youngster, and is now often selected as U18s skipper. Wells is a left-footed centre-back.

1 From which club did the Hammers sign Javier Hernandez in July 2017?

2 Which League Two side were the Hammers paired with in their first EFL Cup tie of the 2017/18 season?

3 Can you name the two youngsters who made their West Ham debuts in the EFL Cup victory over Bolton?

4 Record signing Marko Arnautovic was handed which squad number following his arrival at London Stadium?

5 Who netted his first goal for the club in the EFL Cup triumph over Bolton Wanderers in September 2017?

6 Which Championship club signed Hammers midfielder Robert Snodgrass on loan for the 2017/18 season?

7 Against which club did the Hammers win their first Premier League fixture of the 2017/18 season?

8 Which member of the Hammers' squad scored the first goal of the new 2017/18 season at London Stadium?

9 At what stage of the competition did West Ham United enter the EFL Cup in 2017/18?

10 On which Premier League ground did Joe Hart record his first away clean-sheet of the season?

11 Against which club are the Hammers scheduled to play their final game of 2017?

12 How many Premier League London derbies will the Hammers face in 2017/18?

13 Can you name the two sides that will play Premier League fixtures at London Stadium for the first time in 2017?

14 Pablo Zabaleta joined in the summer from Manchester City, but can you name the Spanish club that City signed him from?

15 Can you name the two players who made their final appearances for West Ham in the final game of last season at Burnley?

16 Goalkeeper Darren Randolph left West Ham United to join which Championship club in the summer of 2017?

17 Who scored West Ham's first Premier League goal of 2017/18?

18 With which club did Hammers' on-loan 'keeper Joe Hart play his first-ever Football League game?

19 What nationality is 2017 summer signing Sead Haksabanovic?

20 2017/18 is Mark Noble's 14th consecutive season of appearing in the Hammers' first team - true or false?

ANSWERS ON PAGE 82

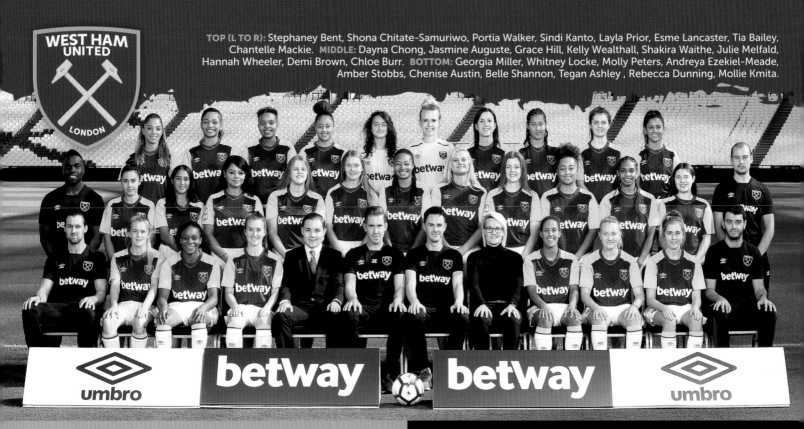

TOP (L TO R): Stephaney Bent, Shona Chitate-Samuriwo, Portia Walker, Sindi Kanto, Layla Prior, Esme Lancaster, Tia Bailey, Chantelle Mackie. **MIDDLE:** Dayna Chong, Jasmine Auguste, Grace Hill, Kelly Wealthall, Shakira Waithe, Julie Melfald, Hannah Wheeler, Demi Brown, Chloe Burr. **BOTTOM:** Georgia Miller, Whitney Locke, Molly Peters, Andreya Ezekiel-Meade, Amber Stobbs, Chenise Austin, Belle Shannon, Tegan Ashley, Rebecca Dunning, Mollie Kmita.

2. CHANTELLE MACKIE

A pacey and attacking minded full-back, Mackie has committed herself to the West Ham ladies for a second season as the side looks to climb through the ranks.

3. JASMINE AUGUSTE

Having moved to West Ham Ladies from Millwall in 2016, Auguste has proven herself to be a tenacious and pacey defender who has grown into a leadership role on the field.

4. AMY COOPER (CAPTAIN)

Named captain for a second successive season, Cooper's energy in midfield and maturity makes her the perfect skipper for the Ladies' side.

5. HANNAH WHEELER

In her third season with the West Ham Ladies, Wheeler is a reliable and composed centre-back who has impressed with her maturity and reliability in the back-line.

6. LEANNE MABEY

A talented and composed defender, Mabey's ability to read developing situations has seen her become a key option for the Irons in their back-line.

7. WHITNEY LOCKE

A home-grown talent, Locke is renowned for her speed and pace, which has been effective both as a striker and on the wing for the Ladies team already.

8. DAYNA CHONG

A talented midfielder, Chong showed her immense ability with a wonderful volleyed goal last season and will hope to continue to show her talent this year.

9. ANDREYA EZEKIEL-MEADE

Stepping up from the U16 Junior Academy team, Ezekiel-Meade is an impressive attacker who also brings assists as well as goals to the side.

10. AMBER STOBBS (VICE CAPTAIN)

Brought in from Everton in the summer, our new No.10 Stobbs brings experience, excitement and creativity to West Ham Ladies' wings and front-line.

11. CHLOE BURR

Formerly of Chelsea, Burr has shown her ability to play either in midfield or as a forward. She finished the campaign as the team's leading goalscorer last season.

12. PAIGE ANDERSON-JAMES

After taking a short break from football, Paige is back scoring goals. Her strength, quick feet and powerful strike will undoubtedly see her lead the Ladies in goals this season.

14. MOLLY PETERS

An exciting young striker, Peters has returned to the West Ham fold to continue her development, show her pace and why she's tough to defend against.

15. SHONA CHITATE-SAMURIWO

A midfield talent, Chitate-Samuriwo is a powerful option in the centre of the park with room to further develop her incredible potential.

16. BELLE SHANNON

A young and talented midfielder who has proven to be a reliable option to bring on in the midfield. Her vision and ability to switch the play provides the team with a different outlook.

17. MOLLIE KMITA

Brought into the side this summer, Kmita has shown her versatility and willingness to learn already this season by featuring in a host of different roles.

18. GEORGIA MILLER

Back at West Ham, Miller is a young and talent midfielder with an eye for a great pass, and the energy to drive into dangerous areas.

19. REBECCA DUNNING

After deciding to join West Ham, last season Rebecca has shown fantastic potential in the midfield. She has tremendous ability to receive the ball in tight areas and retain possession.

20. PORTIA WALKER

Another young and forward-thinking attacking, Portia provides a great option to the team when in possession as she takes players on and looks to link up with centre-forwards.

21. KELLY WEALTHALL

A West Ham Ladies home-grown talent, Wealthall scored an impressive 58 goals in the 2016/17 season in the Essex County Girls League, earning her place in the first team.

22. TIA BAILEY

Now in her second season with the West Ham Ladies having joined from Charlton in 2016, Bailey is a powerful and young defender who has the potential to become a top player.

23. STEPHANEY BENT

Last campaign's Players' Player of the Season, Bent's versatility and determination has seen her become one of West Ham Ladies' top attacking threats since joining last year.

24. DEMI BROWN

Brown is a talented and determined centre-back who loves a strong tackle and has impressed with her composure both with the ball and when winning back possession.

WHU LADIES

25. CHENISE AUSTIN

Signed from Swindon Town in the summer, Austin is a highly-rated defender who can play across the back-line, and brings experience to the side.

26. JULIE MELFALD

Julie joined from Norway where she played at the highest level. A very strong and powerful striker who looks to link up with the midfielders and brings wingers into play with her vision.

27. SHAKIRA WAITHE

A young forward brought in during the summer, Waithe will be hoping to continue her development into a top attacker with West Ham.

28. TEAGAN ASHLEY

A young full-back joining us from Brighton, Teagan will be looking to develop herself and challenge others around her.

29. GRACE HILL

Another young attacker, Hill is looking to build on her progression and continue to show her ability for the first team.

GOALKEEPERS

CHERIE ROWLANDS

An experienced keeper who has played at the very top with Arsenal & Watford. A great distributor who organises the back line, she quickly gained the respect of her peers.

SINDI KANTO

Young goalkeeper who joined on loan from Millwall Lionesses. Sindi has proven herself to be cat like between the posts and will continue to develop under the guidance of peers.

LOTTIE IVISON

Another former Millwall Lioness player, goalkeeper Ivison moved to West Ham in 2016 and has shown excellent composure with the ball and a determination to lead the defence.

LAYLA PRIOR

Joining from a local Essex side, Pior will be looking to establish herself as a strong contender for the starting XI. Her experience and willingness to learn will see her progress quickly.

BILLY BONDS' SIX STEPS TO STARDOM

CONFIRMING HIS STATUS AS A TRUE HAMMERS LEGEND

1

BARGAIN BUY

Ron Greenwood made a wise choice when he invested a fee of £50,000 in Charlton defender Billy Bonds in May 1967.

Ironically Bonds' debut came in Ken Brown's testimonial match, so just as one glittering West Ham career was coming to an end, another was taking off.

The first of Bonds' record 663 league outings for the club came on the opening day of 1967/68 campaign against Sheffield Wednesday.

2

WEMBLEY WINNER

Following the departure of Bobby Moore in 1974, Bonds was handed the captaincy at the Boleyn Ground.

In his first full season as skipper, he led the club to FA Cup glory in 1974/75 as two goals from Alan Taylor preceded Bonds leading the team up the famous Wembley steps to collect the trophy.

He repeated the feat five years later as the Hammers overcame the odds to defeat Arsenal 1-0.

3

PROMOTION-WINNING SKIPPER

After three seasons in the Second Division, Bonds finally led the Hammers back to the big-time as they stormed to the Second Division title in 1980/81.

The title and promotion were secured with a 13-point cushion over runners-up Notts County. The campaign saw Bonds play an incredible 59 games in all competitions - the most he ever achieved in a single season at the club.

5
ACCOLADES GALORE

After over 20 years at the club, Bonds established himself as very much the local hero and had been voted Hammer of the Year on four occasions 1971, 1974, 1975 and 1987.

He was made an MBE in January 1988 and presented with the PFA Merit Award in April 1988 by his fellow professionals.

In May 2013, Bonds became the first recipient of West Ham United's lifetime achievement award.

4
RECORD APPEARANCE MAKER

Bonds played in a colossal 799 games for the Hammers between August 1967 and April 1988.

His club record 799 first team outings combined 787 starts and 12 substitute appearances - he also netted 61 goals for the club. It is extremely unlikely that any player will ever surpass this outstanding record for the club.

6
MANAGING TO SUCCEED

After retiring as a player, Bonds was appointed youth coach by John Lyall, before succeeding Lou Macari as Hammers manager in 1990.

During his time as boss, Bonds twice led the club to promotion to the First Division. He secured promotion in his first full season as the Hammers ended the 1990/91 season as runners-up to Oldham.

They also reached the FA Cup semi-final that season. A second promotion was won in 1992/93.

ANSWERS

PAGE 52 · 2016/2017 SEASON QUIZ

1. Cheikhou Kouyate (v Domzale, Europa League). 2. James Collins
(v Chelsea Away). 3. Bournemouth. 4. Accrington Stanley.
5. Seven. 6. Cheikhou Kouyate and Edimilsom Fernandes. 7. Arsenal.
8. Astra Giurgiu. 9. Crystal Palace, Swansea City and Hull City.
10. Manchester United. 11. Nine. 12. Darren Randolph
(22 versus Adrian's 16). 13. Declan Rice. 14. Reading.
15. Away to Manchester United. 16. Valencia. 17. Spain. 18. Hull City.
19. Manuel Lanzini. 20. Michail Antonio.

PAGE 60 · WORLD CUP QUIZ

1930. Argentina. 1934. Four. 1938. Paris. 1950. USA. 1954. Hungary.
1958 & 1962. Brazil. 1966. Everton's Ray Wilson. 1970. Italy.
1974. The Cruyff turn, after legendary Dutch footballer Johan Cruyff.
1978. Mario Kempes. 1982. Trevor Brooking. 1986. Diego Maradona.
1990. Cameroon. 1994. Russia. 1998. Ronaldo. 2002. Miroslav Klose.
2006. Portugal 1-0 Netherlands. 2010. Matthew Upson.
He tied with Steven Gerrard and Jermain Defoe on one goal each.
2014. Hosts: Brazil. Winners: Germany. 2018. Russia.

PAGE 70 · FAN'TASTIC

Steve Lomas, Alvin Martin, Julian Dicks, Bobby Moore and Billy Bonds.

PAGE 76 · 2017/2018 SEASON QUIZ

1. Bayer Leverkusen. 2. Cheltenham Town. 3. Sead Haksabanovic
and Nathan Holland. 4. Number seven. 5. Arthur Masuaku. 6. Aston Villa.
7. Huddersfield Town. 8. Pedro Obiang. 9. The second round.
10. The Hawthorns. 11. Tottenham Hotspur. 12. Eight (four at home
and four away) v Chelsea, Tottenham Hotspur, Arsenal and Crystal Palace.
13. Huddersfield Town and Brighton & Hove Albion. 14. Espanyol.
15. Sofiane Feghouli and Ashley Fletcher. 16. Middlesbrough.
17. Javier Hernandez. 18. Shrewsbury Town. 19. Swedish. 20. True.